The Candidates 1980

The Candidates 1980

ARAM BAKSHIAN, JR

ARLINGTON HOUSE·PUBLISHERS
NEW ROCHELLE, NEW YORK

Book Design by Michael Yellin

Library of Congress Cataloging in Publication Data
Bakshian, Aram.
   The candidates 1980.

   1.   Presidents—United States—Election—1980.
I.   Title.
JK526 1980.B34   324.973'0926   79-27070
ISBN 0-87000-472-7

Manufactured in the United States of America

To My Family—
six of a kind

"When I was a boy I was told that anybody could become President; I'm beginning to believe . . ."
                                    —*Clarence Darrow*

CONTENTS

INTRODUCTION:

Looking for Leadership

*Knowledge of human nature is the beginning
and end of political education.*
—Henry Adams

HISTORY, AN OLD Viennese friend of mine once told me, is mainly a matter of silly people rediscovering the obvious by tripping over it. He was certainly in a position to know, having lived through the reigns of two emperors, a republic, the Anschluss, the Russian occupation and yet another republic. Through it all, he insisted, the Viennese, for all of the surface alterations of their society and politics, hadn't changed that much from the days when he first came to know the old Imperial city as a young boy in the 1880's until the year of his death in 1975.

Of course Washington is hardly Vienna, and America is hardly Austria—which probably comes as a source of relief to all parties concerned—but many of the supposed innovations in recent American politics are not as innovative as they seem. As a nation, we have always had a passion for the new, or at least for the appearance of newness. But the rise of the caucus, the emergence of one-issue constituencies, the regional shifts in political alignment and strength, and the current stress on ethnic voting blocs all have deep roots in American history. Like so much else in our society, they are recurrent rather than new phenomena. In spite of what H.L. Mencken once described as our voracious national appetite for bogus revelation, the basic current of American society has been a consistent one.

Group by group, region by region, for nearly two centuries now we have tended to vote for those leaders whom we perceive as most likely to protect what we have (materially and, to a lesser extent, spiritually) and, whenever possible, increase our slice of the economic and social pie.

Blue-collar Catholics who voted for Franklin Roosevelt as unemployed young laborers and more than a generation later supported Richard Nixon were consistent in their way. They voted for the New Deal and the welfare state it represented at a time when they needed subsidized work and direct government assistance. In 1968, and even more in 1972, faced with the choice between Nixon and McGovern, they voted for the man they thought would best protect the considerable economic and social progress they had made from a new set of have-nots and extremists who, as they saw it, threatened not only their economic well-being, but also the stability of schools and neighborhoods, national security and many aspects of conventional morality. By their lights, they made the right decision, and many of them, when polled long after Nixon's resignation, still insisted that, given the Nixon-McGovern choice, they would do the same again. Similarly Southern Blacks who, when they were allowed to vote at all, chose the "Party of Lincoln" from the Reconstruction until the New Deal, and then voted overwhelmingly Democratic from the New Deal to the present, have operated with equal consistency and pragmatism.

Individual people, parties and groups have changed places in society; underlying motive forces abide. This does not mean that we are a nation of purely rational voters, for nearly all of us perceive our rational interests through emotionally tinted glasses. Especially in the age of television, individual candidates with "star quality" can divert the public in a way that puzzles the ideologues and disappoints the cold-blooded statisticians. But just as most television series are canceled after one season, this kind of transient charismatic political popularity usually enjoys only a short run. By claiming to be something special on the way in, such candidates—unless they really *are* special—guarantee their own early departure through dashed expectations. Shallow glamour candidates tend to sow the seeds of their own demise, for as Harry Truman once said, "A President needs political understanding to *run* the government, but he may be elected without it."

Generally only once. One need look no further than Jimmy Carter to appreciate the truth of Truman's characteristically pithy warning. The man who talked of giving the American people leadership to match their own lofty idealism in 1976 now complains incessantly about a "new" spirit of national malaise that makes it difficult for him to lead the country in a popular, effective way. But how new is this trend toward fragile, one-term incumbencies?

To paraphrase the irrepressibly oleine Victor Lasky, it didn't start with Carter. Nor for that matter did it start with Watergate. The "new" phenomenon of the hobbled incumbent dates back to the earliest years of the Republic. Of thirty-eight Presidents, only ten (Washington, Jefferson, Madison, Monroe, Jackson, Grant, Cleveland, Wilson, Franklin Roosevelt and Eisenhower) have served two or more full terms in office. And each of these men was either a leader of exceptional stature or, in the cases of Grant and Eisenhower, a popular military hero with a following that transcended party loyalties.

Since the Great Depression which, by pouring over into

World War II, gave Roosevelt a uniquely prolonged basis for emergency leadership that his political skill and magnetism were equal to, only Dwight Eisenhower has served out two full terms in office. And good old Ike, as the latest crop of historical revisionists is beginning to discover (perhaps rediscover would be the better word), was hardly the affably bumbling grandpa that many took him for at the time. In fact, with a minimum of fuss and a fair amount of good will and good luck, Eisenhower gave the United States its only eight years of continuous post-war peace and stability—an era that may yet prove to be the last in the twentieth century when America enjoyed prolonged social peace and progress at home matched by diplomatic peace and prestige abroad.

As for the rest of our post-Rooseveltian Presidents, Truman chose not to run for reelection in 1952 after his own party rebelled and his national popularity had reached an all-time low. John Kennedy, on the eve of his fatal journey to Dallas, was also plunging in the polls. It took the guilt trauma of his assassination to launch the Camelot legend, which has earned his brief and far from stainless Presidency a posthumous place in the national folklore. While Lyndon Johnson always insisted that he bowed out in 1968 for strictly health reasons, he too had reached low ebb in the opinion polls, and with the entry of Robert Kennedy into the race following Eugene McCarthy's strong (46 percent) showing in the New Hampshire primary, Johnson seemed destined to go down the tubes in any event. Nixon, the strangest case of them all, resigned in disgrace over Watergate before completing his second term, while his successor, Jerry Ford, after a close victory over Ronald Reagan at Kansas City, was narrowly defeated by Jimmy Carter, who ran as the embodiment of the "Old Politics" of small-town virtues and of the Roosevelt coalition. A year before the 1980 elections, Carter had already lost the confidence of a large chunk of the nation—so much so that even Ronald Reagan, who couldn't beat Ford for the GOP nomination in 1976, led

Carter in a head-on national preference poll. The same polls showed Reagan in his turn being trounced by Teddy Kennedy almost two to one.

As for innovation, the only new political wrinkle in the 1980 race, maverick Governor Jerry Brown of California, has so far failed to become more than a minor irritant—first to Carter and now, as a potential drain on some of his liberal and "flake" support, to Teddy Kennedy. So much for the new-wave politics some of our social scholars predicted would inundate us from the sunny Southwest.

Reluctantly, one concludes that the more things have changed, the more they have remained the same in American presidential politics. The challenge lies in seeing through the seasonally varying foliage and transient surface shifts to the permanent underlying contours of the political landscape— contours that have changed remarkably little and only very gradually in the post-war era.

Once you look deeply enough, both the seeming changes and the less apparent permanencies of our electoral system begin to make sense. What seem at first glance to be inconsistencies become congruent. And the future, while far from obvious, becomes less opaque. The process is fairly simple but involves five tiers of examination and speculation:

• Fitting the 1980 race for the Presidency into the historical context of American politics and social and economic cycles.
• Measuring the individual candidates (their records, their personalities, their abilities and liabilities) to the needs *and* preferences of their respective parties.
• Handicapping each candidate's chances for actually winning nominations, qualified or not.
• Handicapping presidential candidates and vice presidential selections that stand the best chance of winning the general election next November.

• Assessing which of the potential winners stand the best chance of governing the country well.

Admittedly, at each level many of these judgments must be subjective. The imponderables are many, and the best one can hope for is partial success. But even partial success in applying common-sense analysis and informed speculation to our confused electoral process is, I am convinced, a real step forward from the mix of show-business tinsel, micromaniac obsession with arcane statistics, and philosophical and mystical gaseousness that have too long dominated the field. Lest I be accused of concealing any bias, I hereby confess to an equal loathing for irresponsible gonzo journalists of the Hunter Thompson variety, preachy ritual entrail-readers like Theodore White, hackneyed old-school political reporters who believe in shoe leather as a substitute for, rather than a supplement to, intelligent analysis, and arrogant political "pros" who think they can and should play Pygmalion, transforming any unarticulated lump of political clay they choose into a conquering puppet.

Nor do I agree with the more sentimental conventional wisdom of recent years that Presidents—like gravid guppies—grow in office. The Carter experience would seem to demonstrate the opposite. At least in the public perception, Jimmy Carter has been the incredible shrinking President, a man who looks smaller and smaller the longer one observes him trying to lead. Thomas Jefferson once complained that no man brings out of the Presidency the reputation he carried in. It might be closer to the truth to say that no man takes out of the Presidency qualities he did not bring to the office in the first place. One can learn in office and one can improve one's *technique* through practice. But the courage, cowardice, wisdom, duplicity or folly a person demonstrates in office is rooted in the inner self—the differing character and capability innate in each human being. Events may bring these qualities to the surface, but events do not create them. This makes it all the more important to detect their presence or absence in candidates *before* they become incumbents.

And that brings me to the largest section of this book—my individual assessments of the leading candidates for the Democratic and Republican nominations. I may have treated my subjects too personally, too *ad hominem* for some tastes. My only justification is that it is a man, as much as it is a team or a political party, that occupies the Presidency. *He* (and, perhaps someday soon, she) is the biggest single issue of any presidential campaign. And the candidate's character and personal performance offer one of the best keys we have to future reactions under stress. Allegations of financial scandal, cheated exams, negligent actions that may have cost the lives of others, and the history of serious physical or mental illness are all public concerns when the person involved is seeking the highest office of elective trust in the land. Having said this, let me quickly add that I have done my best to filter facts from rumor and to label as gossip those items with only partial verification. My apologies to those who would have enjoyed a more salacious approach. Throughout, my aim has been to show what kind of people the candidates are, or at least appear to be, from as many different perspectives as possible—as administrators, as thinkers, as communicators, as friends and neighbors, and as individual studies in human personality. I don't pretend to deal in certainties, only likelihoods. Many a cad has charmed his way into high office undetected and many a politician of solid but prosaic worth has bored his way to premature retirement. But the basic question of character remains pivotal, at least from my viewpoint, to Presidential suitability. Without sound character, great ability or popularity can be used as readily for evil as for good.

Anyone who knows me knows that I am not, to put it mildly, a Pollyanna. If anything, thirty-five years in Washington have tended to thicken my skin to minor human foibles. But I do believe in what the British used to call "bottom"—a kind of basic moral solidity, a sound core of moral or ethical standards that can transform a standoffish intellectual like Thomas Jefferson into a great leader or a man of sound but modest attainments like Gerald Ford into a trusted, respected caretaker President. These core values can take many forms, from religious orthodoxy to a humanist respect for the rights of others. My main concern is to separate, where possible, the candidates with such a solid moral core from the hollow men whom one encounters with such alarming frequency in politics. When the arena is left to the latter, real leadership is lost, and the best to be hoped for is a clever demagogue of the type Theodore Roosevelt described—one who "says what everybody is thinking most often and in the loudest voice." Our century has already heard enough such shouting.

In a nutshell then, my aim is to show not only who is running for President but why, and to handicap their individual chances for mounting successful races *and* successful administrations. This raises the rather obvious question of who I am and what qualifications I bring to the job. As a native Washingtonian, I have been a close observer of politics all of my life. Latterly, I have also been a political practitioner on a fairly high level as a speechwriter to two Presidents during three and a half years as a White House aide, as a special assistant to a Secretary of the Treasury and a chairman of the Republican National Committee, as a legislative assistant to a member of Congress, as a professional participant in the last three presidential elections and as a lecturing fellow at the Institute of Politics, Kennedy School of Government, Harvard University.

My own historical writing on subjects as diverse as Edwardian England and the American Revolution, and my many essays and reviews in journals including the *Wall Street Journal, History Today,* the *New York Times, National Review,* the American and English *Spectators, National Observer, Washingtonian Magazine* and various international editions of *Reader's Digest* may already be familiar to some of you. To those reading me for the first time, I can only say that I have made every effort at critical objectivity in assessing the candidates as men and as politicians. And assessing candidates, in one form or another, has been my principal vocation for most of my adult life. To that extent, I remain a political insider, although I have made it a point to withhold my endorsement and my professional services from any of the potential 1980 candidates while writing this book. As far as the battle for the 1980 nomination is concerned, I have maintained a state of armed neutrality, but despite my noncombatant status, my contacts with a number of the candidates and their campaign staffs have given me access to information and planning sessions that would ordinarily be closed to writers or journalists.

Like most Americans, my first reaction when the early campaign articles and television spots started appearing in the autumn of 1979 was, "Oh God, not another presidential race!" To me politics has always been a necessary and occasionally interesting evil—civil business that must be attended to not because it is conducive to good company, good digestion or good times, but because it is, as Charles de Gaulle once said to Clement Attlee, too serious a matter to be left to the politicians. If honest, able citizens drop out of the process and the voting booth because of apathy or despair, the field is left clear to the power brokers, the extremists and the opportunists. We have enough of them as it is. So, since there is going to be a presidential election in 1980 whether I look forward to it or not, I decided to apply whatever insight and experience I might have in a way that the voting public might find useful and entertaining.

I must confess at the outset that I am not all that impressed with the candidate class of 1980. Some of the most qualified presidential material in both parties is, as of this writing, either out of the running by choice or very much in the underdog category. But even mediocrity has its gradations and, within these limits, I echo Jimmy Carter's rallying cry (but not his choice) from 1976: "Why not the best?"

As this book goes to press, and throughout the long months leading to November of 1980, the political crescendo will build. The journalists, lobbyists, flacks and candidates—mercenaries and idealists alike—will swarm like locusts from caucuses to primaries to conventions across the country. But despite the escalated barrage of balloons, promises, charges and countercharges, if the steady trend of the last twenty-six years holds true, a smaller proportion of eligible voters than ever will cast the crucial ballots in November. From 61.9 percent of eligible voters in 1964 the rate steadily declined to 54.3 percent in 1976 and an all-time low of 35.2 percent for the mid-term congressional elections in 1978. Of those who do vote in 1980, many will do so without enthusiasm and some with considerable trepidation about both of the candidates they must choose between. Yet a great many of the key factors that will lead up to that final choice are predictable. Dangerous trends spotted in time can be modified or reversed. Favorable trends can be strengthened. So I have risked making as many predictions as reasonably possible (often in the form of alternate scenarios rather than single, ironclad certainties) about *The Candidates 1980,* as well as trying to give the reader a feel for the men and the issues involved.

Plato defined democracy as "a charming form of government, full of variety and disorder." So it remains. Its survival, like that of all political systems, depends on leaders and citizens capable of choosing wisely and living reasonably with the results, avoiding what historian Will Durant has warned is the potential fate of any society: death "by excess of its basic principles." For too long American political life has suffered from an excess of excesses—an understandable but dangerous emotional orgy after the Kennedy and King assassinations, an excess of callousness on the part of apologists for the abuse of presidential powers, an excess of hypocritical political opportunism on the part of those who stood to gain from the shambles and paralysis of Watergate, and an excess of apathy on the part of nonspecial interest, nonextremist citizens who grumble about government abuses and mismanagement from the sidelines. Camelot fantasies, Vietnam, the Imperial Presidency, Watergate, the intractable Congress, and superficially attractive media candidates who prove inadequate in office have left us in a fine mess.

But there is plenty of room left for hope and even more for amusement in the unfolding political melodrama if we bother to sift the rubble for valuables. Every presidential campaign is a sort of civic scavenger hunt, rich in heroes, sharpers, clowns, patriots, weaklings, sages and potential accidents of history. Most of them are far from ideal presidential material, but nearly all of them are interesting and, in one way or another, sympathetic characters. And each is a reflection of some part of our national heritage and an intimation of some part of our political future, to be ignored at peril. Happy hunting.

Washington, D.C.
December 1979   Aram Bakshian, Jr.

PART I

The View from the Starting Gate

Political campaigns are designedly made into emotional orgies which endeavor to distract attention from the real issues involved, and they actually paralyze what slight powers of cerebration man can normally muster.
—James Harvey Robinson

BY NOVEMBER 4, 1979, exactly a year before election day 1980, the future was already now. Officially or unofficially, all of the major candidates and most of the long shots were at the starting gate, and Democratic National Committee Chairman John White was predicting that the battle for the nomination would provide not only "lots of excitement" but, in the case of the strife-torn Democratic Party, "a big train wreck." Tip O'Neill, the Falstaffian Speaker of the House and a longtime Kennedy booster, reluctantly agreed that if Teddy Kennedy succeeded in beating Carter out of the nomination, it would lead to "an s.o.b. of an election." On the Republican side, while passions as usual were a bit more muted, a crowded field of challengers had taken on Ronald Reagan, the aging frontrunner. As the campaign progressed, tensions inevitably mounted. On both sides, the horse race threatened to degenerate into a catfight.

Everything seemed to have started early. Even the sage turf accountants of Ladbrokes, England's premier bookie chain, had already posted political odds: Teddy Kennedy seven-to-four over Jimmy Carter for the Democratic nomination, but if Carter should make it through the Convention, Jimmy Carter two-to-one over whomever the Republicans might run against him. Most political pros in Washington tended to agree.

For the spiritually minded, the early psychic and occult predictions were also available, more notable for extravagance than consistency. Amidst dire prophecies concerning Ryan O'Neal's mental health, Liz Taylor's marital bliss, Dolly Parton's weight problems (the latter two categories being interchangeable) and Debby Boone's impending motherhood, assorted clairvoyants, satanists and astrologers predicted Carter, Kennedy, Connally or Baker victories. One prudent Washington seeress solemnly assured her public that the next President of the United States would be a man who "was born in February"—a flexible formula that just happens to accommodate three of the most promising candidates in the race: Teddy Kennedy, John Connally and Ronald Reagan. Meanwhile Ms. Sybil Leek, a self-proclaimed English witch, was willing to be more specific, flatly declaring that "an Aquarian" would be elected in 1980—which could be either Ronald Reagan or Representative John Anderson, the darkest of dark horses, Aquarianism aside.

But if one witch's opinion counts for anything, what about a witch-wide consensus? Under the auspices of the aptly-located New York Center for the Strange, a survey of 285 practicing American witches and warlocks tapped Jimmy Carter as the favorite for reelection after a "no-holds-barred" party contest with Teddy Kennedy. Having disposed of the White House a year early, the same group went on to predict that Richard Nixon would rise yet again from his political coffin to run for the Senate in New York, a sex scandal would topple the puritanical regime of the Ayatollah Khomeini in Iran, Vice

President Mondale would "make a startling announcement," and—most striking of all—an elderly gentleman found adrift in a raft on the Atlantic "will claim to be a survivor of the Titanic."

So much for the spirit world. To return to the fleshier but only slightly less bizarre realm of politics, a year before the 1980 elections both major parties had incumbents of sorts—men with a moral or tradition-bound claim to special consideration in the nominating process. The Democrats had Jimmy Carter, a sitting President whose popularity was seriously eroded but who still wielded the power, the patronage and the ability to direct events and command headlines that are unique to the White House. In the Republican column, Ronald Reagan, the slightly rusty Paladin of the Right, also enjoyed the advantages and disadvantages of a kind of pseudo-incumbency. From the moment Jimmy Carter defeated Jerry Ford, Reagan had been the unofficial banner bearer of his party, the only man with a nationwide network of supporters, volunteers, contributors and professional organizers dedicated to his nomination—a national force actually in place and working since 1976.

In their respective parties, Carter and Reagan were definitely the men to beat, the targets every other candidate for the nomination had to aim at, regardless of week-to-week fluctuations in the polls. But both were—and are—highly vulnerable. What makes them different from their rivals is not so much their strength as the fact that their rejection, more than any of their competitors, could inflict deep internal wounds on their parties and give birth to splits that could change the course of the election. If Carter is balked of the Democratic nomination, his victor will have to run in November with one eye on his Republican opponent and the other on a hostile, embittered White House. A Carter defeat could also mean the rebirth of the GOP's moribund Southern Strategy, with most of the states of the old Confederacy choosing even a moderately conservative Republican over a liberal Democratic candidate like Kennedy or Brown who had turned out an incumbent southern President.

As for Reagan, if he loses the Republican nomination, especially to an allegedly more liberal challenger, the cost to the party could be enormous in terms of lost grassroots volunteers, most of whom tend to be conservative. And in the general election, the loss could be even greater in terms of conservative Democratic and independent voters in the crucial South and Southwest.

Nevertheless, there were plenty of challengers on both sides and at least one of them, Teddy Kennedy, had an even or better chance of beating his party's incumbent. That much was already clear in November of 1979 when, barring scandal, illness, assassination or the second coming, all of the principal entries were in place at the starting gate.

From the beginning, the star media attraction was Teddy Kennedy, Camelot's heir apparent. The moment his intention to run was leaked, he was recognized as the only serious intraparty threat facing Carter. The best that Jerry Brown could hope for was to play pilot fish to Teddy's shark. The Republican runners were less easily ranked. After Reagan came a distinct middle field of three major declared contenders. "Big John" Connally, the personally imposing former Lyndon Johnson protégé and Texas governor who, having served as Richard Nixon's Treasury Secretary, switched parties to run as a born again Republican, is a formidable presence on the stump with strong business support and a correspondingly lush war chest. What Connally lacked at the outset was proven voter strength among registered Republicans and local party workers, the men and women who must ultimately choose the nominee. His may be a top-heavy candidacy, "all sail and no anchor," as Lord Macaulay might have put it.

Second of the midfield trio is Senate Minority Leader Howard Baker of Tennessee. Baker is a stable, highly intelligent legislator with a skilled parliamentarian's mind and manner-isms. A good "cool" presence on the tube, Baker is, if anything, a little too glib and conciliatory, never quite seeming to make a clear stand when his addiction to senatorial courtesies and orotundities gets the better of him. Organizationally Baker has also been a slow starter with a reputation for sloppy staff work. Of Reagan's major challengers, he is perhaps the most eligible as a proven Republican elective official. But he has also been the most sluggish organizer and the candidate most reluctant to roll up his sleeves and campaign with the hoi polloi. This is a necessary if distasteful tactic in nomination politics, espe-cially in New Hampshire, where a pampered primary elector-ate expects to be personally petted, coaxed and cajoled, not merely appealed to via radio, television and billboards.

Last of the major Reagan challengers is George Bush, whose elective record is weak (two terms as a House member from Texas and two unsuccessful runs for the Senate). But Bush's general record of public service is impressive. He has been U.S. Ambassador to the United Nations, Chairman of the Republi-can National Committee, the first American envoy to Commu-nist China, and Director of the CIA. Bush is bright, articulate and an energetic campaigner, with some of the top profes-sional organizers in his camp. His big problem as of November 4, 1979 was name recognition. Known and respected by Wash-ington insiders, party regulars and journalists, George Bush was still a virtual unknown with the general public.

Behind the big three trailed four officially declared long-shots: Senator Bob Dole of Kansas, Jerry Ford's saturnine run-ning mate in 1976, but so far a man without a demonstrable national electoral base and a candidate unable to raise suffi-cient funds to carve one out; Representatives Phil Crane and John Anderson of Illinois, the Tweedledum and Tweedledee of the GOP's congressional right and left wings, respectively; the omnipresent, politically punchdrunk Mr. Harold Stassen, a failed Republican Wunderkind of the late 1940's who won't—

or can't—stop running for President and whose sole companion on the campaign trail these days is a painfully frayed toupee; and finally, the enigmatic Mr. Ben Fernandez, a wealthy but obscure Mexican-American businessman of the self-made variety. Mr. Fernandez has gone Abraham Lincoln one better. Honest Abe may have been born in a log cabin; Ben Fernandez was born in a boxcar. One can't help feeling a touch of whimsical affection for this Hispanic Horatio Alger, but treating his candidacy seriously is another matter. To date the Fernandez victory strategy consists of taking the nation by storm after a landslide win in the February 17th Republican Primary in Puerto Rico (!)—the earliest and probably least relevant of all GOP primaries. An imaginative approach, this, but not, one fears, the key to a Fernandez Presidency.

Two much more formidable potential contenders still waited in the Republican wings in November of 1979. Both men deserved to be taken seriously as presidential material if not as candidates. Former President Gerald Ford, who had let it be known that he was "available" but would not actively seek the nomination, might still be the man for the GOP to turn to in a convention deadlock—a remote possibility at best, but stranger things have happened. Ford, with all his limitations, had at least proven that he was capable of *being* President. No great shakes, perhaps, but an experienced and reasonably steady hand at the helm. In a bitter stalemate, Ford could offer war-weary delegates a way out.

Also waiting in the wings in November was General Alexander Haig, respected former NATO commander in Europe, serene White House chief of staff in the last harried months of the Nixon Administration and able former head of the National Security Council. Like Ford, Haig had proven his ability to exercise leadership once he was placed in authority, but he remained an unknown quantity as a seeker of elective power, an unproven campaigner. With Haig there was another important "if" as well. He might opt to run for the Senate in his native Pennsylvania rather than become seriously embroiled in the presidential race. Skeptics dismissed him as a scaled-down clone of the late Dwight Eisenhower. Haig, they claimed, was a political general who had excelled at neither politics nor war. But most of those who have worked with him (as I had the opportunity of doing for several years in the White House) take Alexander Haig seriously as a leader of character, an intellect and an administrator. These, while admirable qualities in a President, are not necessarily the stuff of which good candidates are made.

The candidates at the starting gate. There are no certainties in politics—one of the few intriguing things about an often seamy business. But it is as near a certainty as anything in politics can be that one of these fourteen men (eight, really, once one has discounted Brown, Dole, Crane, Anderson, Stassen and Fernandez as serious prospects) will be the next President of the United States.

But before we examine each of these men separately and at length, we should take a look at the political terrain—the obstacle course lying between each runner and victory. Not for nothing did political reporter Jules Witcover call his massive study of the 1976 presidential race *Marathon.* For sheer grueling exertion, the race for the White House has no equal in the history of representative government. And, if anything, the party reforms and proliferating caucuses and primaries of recent years—taken in combination with ever-increasing media demands on candidates—have rendered the course even more hazardous and demanding.

A quick glimpse at the two "Obstacle Course Calendars" that follow gives a shorthand idea of the incredible job facing each of the candidates and his campaign team. Especially crucial events are printed in capital letters, but in a close race, any of them could spell the difference between victory and defeat. The tighter the race becomes, the more important even the smallest district or county caucus can be in the scramble for a majority of the 3,331 Democratic and 1,993 Republican delegates at stake.

Despite the profusion of opportunities this long obstacle course offers those voters interested in helping to choose a presidential nominee, it would be wrong to assume that caucus, convention and primary balloting will result in anything close to a representative sampling of public sentiment. The nominating process is riddled with too many intentional distortions for that. Many key primary states, whether important because of their dramatic timing or the number of delegates at stake, are radically atypical of national norms. And even in big, representative states with a balance of urban, suburban and rural voters, low turnout virtually guarantees that activists, hard-core party "regulars," one-issue pressure groups, and union and professional interests will play an unduly large role in nominating, as opposed to electing, the next President.

Nineteen-seventy-six was a good case in point. Even in New Hampshire, where participation in the presidential primary is a source of local pride (and one of the few free forms of amusement during the bleak northern winter), only 32.6 percent of voting-age citizens bothered to cast a primary ballot in 1976. And the 187,312 voters who did scattered their support amidst a long string of candidates ranging from the far right to the far left. There were tactical winners and losers in the 1976 New Hampshire Primary, but there was no clear consensus among the voters.

In other important primary states, the turnout was even worse: 27 percent in Illinois, 28.3 percent in Michigan, 27.9 percent in Ohio, 20.7 percent in North Carolina and an abysmal 11.7 percent in New Jersey. In twenty-eight primaries held across the country in 1976—and with both the Republican and Democratic nominations hotly contested—an average of less than a third of the elegible electorate (28 percent) participated.

REPUBLICAN CANDIDATES' OBSTACLE COURSE CALENDAR
January—June 1980
(Key events in capital letters)

January 21st: *Iowa* Republicans hold precinct caucuses to select delegates to county-wide party conventions.

January 29th: *Hawaii* GOP precincts select delegates to state GOP convention.

February 1st: *Maine* GOP begins series of municipal caucuses ending March 15th.

February 2nd: *Arkansas* GOP congressional district committees select district delegates.

February 16th: *Arkansas* GOP state committee elects at-large delegates.

February 17th: *Puerto Rico* GOP Primary (first of the season).

February 26th: NEW HAMPSHIRE PRIMARY.
Minnesota GOP precinct caucuses select delegates to county conventions.

March 1st: *Iowa* GOP holds county conventions to select delegates to district and state conventions.

March 4th: *Massachusetts* Primary.
Vermont Primary.

March 8th: SOUTH CAROLINA PRIMARY.

March 10th: *Minnesota* GOP begins county conventions to select delegates to district and state conventions (through April 2nd).

March 11th: FLORIDA PRIMARY.
Alabama Primary.
Georgia Primary.
Washington caucuses.

March 18th: ILLINOIS PRIMARY

March 24th: *Florida* GOP leaders select district delegates.

March 25th: *Connecticut* Primary.

March 29th: *Florida* GOP state party committee selects at-large delegates.

April 1st: WISCONSIN PRIMARY.
Kansas Primary.

April 5th: *Louisiana* Primary.

April 7th: *Oklahoma* GOP precinct caucuses select delegates to county conventions.

April 18th: *Maine* GOP state convention (through April 20th).

	Minnesota GOP congressional district conventions (through May 10th).
April 19th:	*Oklahoma* GOP county conventions.
	Alaska GOP State Convention (through April 20th).
April 22nd:	**PENNSYLVANIA PRIMARY.**
May 3rd:	**TEXAS GOP PRIMARY.**
	Oklahoma GOP district conventions to select delegates.
May 5th:	*Colorado* GOP precinct caucuses.
May 6th:	**INDIANA PRIMARY.**
	TENNESSEE PRIMARY.
	NORTH CAROLINA PRIMARY.
	District of Columbia Primary.
May 10th:	*Wyoming* GOP state convention.
May 13th:	*Maryland* Primary.
	Nebraska Primary.
May 15th:	*Colorado* GOP county conventions begin (through June 4th).
May 16th:	*Hawaii* GOP state convention and district caucuses.
May 19th:	*Utah* GOP district meetings held to select delegates to county conventions.
May 20th:	**MICHIGAN PRIMARY.**
	OREGON PRIMARY.
May 27th:	*Idaho* Primary.
	Kentucky Primary.
	Nevada Primary.
May 29th:	*Minnesota* GOP state convention (through May 31st).
May 30th:	*Missouri* GOP state convention (through May 31st).
May 31st:	*Oklahoma* GOP state convention.
June 3rd:	**CALIFORNIA PRIMARY.**
	OHIO PRIMARY.
	NEW JERSEY PRIMARY.
	New Mexico Primary.
	West Virginia Primary.
	Rhode Island Primary.
	Montana Primary.
	South Dakota Primary.
	Mississippi GOP Primary.
June 6th:	*Iowa* GOP state and district conventions (through June 7th).
June 27th:	*Utah* GOP state convention.

DEMOCRATIC CANDIDATES' OBSTACLE COURSE CALENDAR
January—July 1980

January 21st: *Iowa* Democrats hold precinct caucuses to select delegates to county-wide party conventions.

February 10th: *Maine* Democrats hold municipal caucuses.

February 26th: *NEW HAMPSHIRE* PRIMARY.
Minnesota Democratic precinct caucuses select delegates to county caucuses.

March 4th: *Massachusetts* Primary.
Vermont Primary.

March 8th: *Iowa* Democratic county caucuses

March 11th: *FLORIDA* PRIMARY.
Alabama Primary.
Georgia Primary.
Hawaii Democratic precinct meetings.
Oklahoma Democratic caucuses.
Washington Democratic caucuses.
Delaware Democratic district meetings (through May 1st).

March 15th: *Minnesota* Democratic county conventions (through March 30th).

March 16th: *Puerto Rico* Democratic Primary (tentative date).

March 18th: *ILLINOIS* PRIMARY.

March 24th: *South Carolina* Democratic county conventions.

March 25th: *Connecticut* Primary.

March 29th: *Oklahoma* Democratic county conventions.

April 1st: *WISCONSIN* PRIMARY.
Kansas Primary.

April 5th: *Louisiana* Primary.

April 12th: *Arizona* Democratic district and county caucuses.
Virginia Democratic district conventions (through May 3rd).

April 19th: *Iowa* Democratic district conventions.
Oklahoma Democratic district caucuses.
Minnesota Democratic district conventions (through May 4th).

April 22nd: *PENNSYLVANIA* PRIMARY.

May 3rd: *Oklahoma* Democratic state convention (through May 4th).

May 5th: *Colorado* Democratic precinct caucuses.

May 6th:	*INDIANA* PRIMARY. *NORTH CAROLINA* PRIMARY. *TENNESSEE* PRIMARY. *District of Columbia* Primary.
May 10th:	*Wyoming* Democratic state convention.
May 13th:	*MARYLAND* PRIMARY. *Nebraska* Primary.
May 15th:	*Colorado* Democratic county conventions (through June 4th).
May 16th:	*Virginia* Democratic state convention (through May 17th). *Maine* Democratic state convention.
May 19th:	*Utah* Democrats hold district meetings to select delegates to county conventions.
May 20th:	*MICHIGAN* PRIMARY. *OREGON* PRIMARY.
May 24th:	*Delaware* Democratic state convention.
May 27th:	*Kentucky* Primary *Arkansas* Democratic Primary. *Idaho* Primary. *Nevada* Primary.
June 1st:	*Hawaii* Democratic state convention.
June 3rd:	*CALIFORNIA* PRIMARY. *OHIO* PRIMARY. *NEW JERSEY* PRIMARY. *WEST VIRGINIA* PRIMARY. *South Dakota* Primary. *Rhode Island* Primary. *New Mexico* Primary. *Montana* Primary. *Missouri* Primary.
June 6th:	*Minnesota* Democratic state convention (through June 8th).
June 14th:	*Colorado* Democratic state convention. *Iowa* Democratic state convention. *Missouri* Democratic state convention.
June 20th:	*TEXAS* DEMOCRATIC STATE CONVENTION (through June 21st).
June 23rd:	*Virgin Islands* Democratic caucuses.
July —*:	*Utah* Democratic state convention.

*Date of Utah convention still to be determined at time of printing.

Given the low turnout in the 1978 congressional and state elections, the downward spiral can be expected to continue or, at best, to stabilize. Some Kennedy backers insist that the old Camelot magic could make a difference in 1980 by bringing out a bigger chunk of low-participating groups such as young voters, Latins and Blacks, but so far this is a hope rather than a likelihood.

Size of turnout is not the only way of predicting candidate strengths in 1980. We already have some fairly sound indicators of which voter groups will play a disproportionately large or small role in the nominating process. The young, the Blacks and the less educated have stayed away by droves in nearly every recent contest for the nomination. And there are other divisions by race, region and religious and professional patterns that can be expected to vote according to trend. Who are these voters? One guide is an analysis of the 1976 presidential vote along social lines by the editors of the *National Journal,* probably the most meticulously thorough and objective political publication in the country. According to the *National Journal,* there is a clearly contrasting and yet complementary pattern to Republican and Democratic voters. In 1976, the Democratic vote broke down as follows:

21 percent WASP (White Anglo-Saxon Protestant)
17 percent southern White
19 percent Catholic
15 percent Black
4 percent Jewish
22 percent Union Member
2 percent "other"

The Republican vote in 1976 represented an inverted version of the same social mix:

38 percent WASP
24 percent southern White

15 percent Catholic
1   percent Black
1   percent Jewish
15 percent Union Member
6   percent "other"

The differences between these two voter profiles are interesting, but their similarities are even more so. While Blacks and Jews as groups remain steadfastly Democratic by a wide margin, other elements of the old New Deal coalition have become much more fluid. The Republicans enjoyed substantial Union Member and Catholic support in 1976, and more White southern support than might have been expected with a Georgian heading the Democratic ticket. Similarly, the Democrats made substantial inroads into the traditionally Republican stronghold of WASPdom.

Party strength by *region* in 1976 presented a more clear-cut configuration: Jerry Ford carried all of the Northwest and all of the Southwest except for Texas. Carter was equally successful in the old South (except for Virginia) and in all of the big northeastern states except New Jersey. The one major region where the outcome was mixed was the Midwest. In important Midwest states, where WASP, Catholic and blue-collar influence (the three groups that seem to be breaking out of their traditional fixed allegiances) are strongest, Carter carried Minnesota, Wisconsin and Ohio. Ford carried Illinois, Michigan and Indiana. In most cases the victory margins were slim, further reflecting the breakup of strong class, ethnic and religious voting patterns in this part of the country.

On balance, given essentially the same political alignments (or lack of them) in 1980, the Midwest—the quintessential "Middle America" of the social scholars—could once again be the most hotly contested and most pivotal electoral region in both the nominating *and* electoral processes. The other region with swing potential in 1980 is the South, especially in the

November general election. In 1960, 1964 and 1968 presidential elections, the once solidly Democratic South gave most or all of its electoral votes to Republican or third-party candidates. In 1972 Richard Nixon carried the entire South. Jimmy Carter, as a favorite son from the area, temporarily reversed the GOP's winning trend in the South. He would have a hard time repeating that performance in 1980, when even the switch of a few southern states could make all the difference. And a liberal Kennedy or Brown candidacy would almost automatically drive most of the South into the hands of any moderate-to-conservative candidate the Republicans might nominate.

In the 1980 nominating process itself, the South has two important functions. On the Democratic side, it offers an acid test of Jimmy Carter's ability to hold the support he received in 1976 from southern Blacks and southern Democrats in general. If he can't cling to his base in his home region, his prospects for renomination elsewhere must be pretty hopeless. On the Republican side, the South, traditionally the heart of conservative GOP strength, could be the major testing ground for Ronald Reagan.

If Reagan is vulnerable with some conservative Republican voters as well as with his party's minuscule liberal wing, then rivals like Connally, Baker, Bush and Crane should all make serious inroads into the Californian's strength in the South. A poorer than expected Reagan showing in early southern primaries, including South Carolina, Florida, Alabama and Georgia, could mark the beginning of the end for the GOP frontrunner.

A year before the election, and nearly four months before the New Hampshire Primary, both the Democrats and the Republicans already had three premonitory straws (or straw votes) to clutch at—one from the Midwest, one from the South and one from New England. Each was unimportant in itself, but each gave at least an early reading of how effectively indi-

vidual candidates' organizers—if not the candidates themselves—had been doing their jobs.

On October 13, 1979, Florida Democrats held a series of
county caucuses to select delegates to a state-wide party convention. As veteran political reporter, David Broder, remarked a few weeks before this first feeble shot of the nomination war, "On both the Carter and the Kennedy sides, the
October 13 caucuses are being treated as the first battleground
of 1980—even though they have nothing to do with choosing
delegates to the national convention next August." A nonevent
had become national news thanks to heavy media coverage
and the desire of both the Carter and the Draft Kennedy
forces for a dramatic early showing. But once the Florida caucuses *had* been inflated by the flacks, they did become important—not as a test of genuine popular opinion in Florida, but
as a test of Carter and Kennedy organizational competence.

The result was a nominal victory for Carter which actually
betrayed more weakness than strength. Despite outspending
the Kennedy forces $250,000 to $175,000 (not to mention $100
million in tax dollars, the price tag for dropping plans to shift
a naval training base from Pensacola, Florida to Fort Rucker,
Alabama in order to make friends for the Administration in
Florida), Carter was hard-pressed to beat Kennedy in crucial
Dade County. State officials estimated that approximately 2
percent of eligible Democratic voters participated in the caucuses which—Administration pork barrelling aside—means
that between them the Kennedy and Carter forces spent over
ten dollars a head for ballots that would only partially determine a nonbinding straw vote having nothing to do with the
real contest for Florida's nominating delegates. The latter will
be chosen in the statewide primary on March 11, 1980, regardless of local caucus and convention outcomes.

Far more ominous for Carter than Kennedy's strong showing in the Fort Lauderdale and Miami caucusing was the result
of an October 14th newspaper poll of registered Florida

Democrats that gave Kennedy a 52 percent to 27 percent lead over Carter in overall leadership ability. If that kind of voter estimate of the two men holds through to March of 1980, Carter could lose the Florida Primary. All in all then, the Democrats' first test match in Florida had resulted in cold comfort for Jimmy Carter.

Half a continent away, on October 15, 1979, the final figures were released for five straw polls taken at Iowa Republican fundraising events. All five had been won by George Bush, with an overall plurality of 36 percent. As in Florida, these polls had no direct bearing on the ultimate distribution of Iowa's delegates to the National Convention. But they were a small but telling indication of the superiority of a field organization that managed to push the relatively obscure Bush ahead of frontrunner Reagan, John Connally, regional candidate Bob Dole and other GOP contenders. As a test of organization, as opposed to general candidate popularity, the Iowa straw votes were far from meaningless.

All the more so when taken in conjunction with another GOP straw vote held on November 3rd in Portland, Maine. Senator Howard Baker, newly announced as a candidate and carrying the endorsement of Maine's popular Republican Senator William Cohen, was expected to win in Maine. But once again it was George Bush who led the field. Straws in the wind perhaps, but in both tests the wind seemed to be blowing in the same direction—not in favor of the most famous candidates (for Bush consistently trailed Baker, Connally and Reagan in name recognition and most popularity polls) but in favor of the one with the best organized campaign staff. And in a nomination race that most citizens will sit out, this clue to organizational superiority could mean a great deal in the quest for real delegates to the real convention. The following chart, divided by state and party, shows where those delegates are to be found:

WHERE THE DELEGATES ARE IN 1980

State	Democratic Dels.	Republican Dels.
ALABAMA	45	27
ALASKA	11	19
ARIZONA	29	28
ARKANSAS	33	19
CALIFORNIA	306	168
COLORADO	40	31
CONNECTICUT	54	35
DELAWARE	14	12
DISTRICT OF COLUMBIA	19	14
FLORIDA	100	51
GEORGIA	63	36
HAWAII	19	14
IDAHO	17	21
ILLINOIS	179	102
INDIANA	80	54
IOWA	50	37
KANSAS	37	32
KENTUCKY	50	27
LOUISIANA	51	30
MAINE	22	21
MARYLAND	59	30
MASSACHUSETTS	111	42
MICHIGAN	141	82
MINNESOTA	75	34
MISSISSIPPI	32	22
MISSOURI	77	37
MONTANA	19	20
NEBRASKA	24	25
NEVADA	12	17
NEW HAMPSHIRE	19	22
NEW JERSEY	113	66
NEW MEXICO	20	22

NEW YORK	282	123
NORTH CAROLINA	69	40
NORTH DAKOTA	14	17
OHIO	161	77
OKLAHOMA	42	34
OREGON	39	29
PENNSYLVANIA	185	83
RHODE ISLAND	23	13
SOUTH CAROLINA	37	25
SOUTH DAKOTA	19	22
TENNESSEE	55	32
TEXAS	152	80
UTAH	20	21
VERMONT	12	19
VIRGINIA	64	51
WASHINGTON	58	37
WEST VIRGINIA	35	18
WISCONSIN	75	34
WYOMING	11	19
GUAM	4	4
PUERTO RICO	41	14
VIRGIN ISLANDS	4	4
U.S. CITIZENS ABROAD	4	—
LATIN AMERICA (EX-CANAL ZONE)	4	—
TOTAL DELEGATES	3,331	1,993
NEEDED TO WIN NOMINATION	1,666	997

Which two men will win the necessary majorities? In my
Introduction I suggested that the first step to answering that
question was to fit the 1980 race and runners into the historical
context of American politics and social and economic cycles.
Once we understand the patient's state of mind, his actions—
both present and future—begin to make sense.

A brief look at recent electoral trends in the rest of the
democratic West show us that, throughout the developed free
world, the pendulum is swinging to the right—not with exces-
sive speed or force, but with a surprising consistency. Canada
has elected its first Tory government since 1963; conservative-
centrist Giscard d'Estaing has turned back a combined Com-
munist-Socialist bid in France; the newly-freed Spanish electorate has increased its support of the ruling anti-socialist
Union of the Democratic Center; center-right forces were the
biggest winners in the Common Market's first European Parliamentary elections; Swedish voters, for the second time in
three years, have denied power to the traditionally dominant
socialists; Australia, New Zealand and Japan remain in conservative hands; Italy's Christian Democrats have held their
ground while the Communist Party has lost support; and, in
Great Britain, Margaret Thatcher has led the Conservative
Party to victory over Labour with the biggest winning margin
of any British election since 1945.

It's a bad time for most parties of the left in the western
democracies. And in many of these countries, the decisive
issues have had a curiously American ring to them—inflation,
taxes, national security and a rebellion against too much government at too high a price. To the extent that this global
trend applies in America in 1980, the Democrats have plenty
to worry about, no matter whom they nominate and whether
they hold the White House or not.

Ours is not a purely parliamentary system. American presidents of one party have been elected by wide popular margins
at the same time that opposition congressional and state candidates swamped the rest of their ticket—especially when the

president in question was charismatic or managed to run on generalities and rhetoric. It could happen again in 1980. But, even if Carter or Kennedy is elected President, the GOP should make substantial gains in the House of Representatives, the Senate and in state and local races, all of which have been targeted by Republican National Chairman Bill Brock for a major party offensive.

Party labels aside, the American electorate of 1980 and the decade ahead is one with a heavy tilt to middle-class, moderately conservative prejudices and values. The same post-war baby boom that made the late sixties and early seventies so sensitive to the Cult of Youth guarantees that the 1980s will be dominated by young and early middle-aged working adults— the 25- to 50-year-old bracket which already represents nearly a third of the population and will rise to more than 37 percent of it by the decade's end. Reinforcing the age and social outlook of the 1980s, population shifts will continue to strengthen the political clout of the suburbs and the Sunbelt at the expense of the old (and predominantly Democratic) big cities of the Northeast and industrialized Midwest.

The so-called Catholic vote illustrates this shift in microcosm. In 1960, given the chance to put a coreligionist in the White House (and avenge the ghost of wronged Al Smith), a massive Catholic vote helped elect John Kennedy. In 1980 it is far less likely to materialize for Teddy Kennedy. Once almost monolithically Democratic, the Catholic vote in 1980 is more fragmented than at any time in its past. Far from being one bloc, it is now broken up into at least four distinct—and often conflicting—fragments:

• *OLD-LINE BLUE COLLAR CATHOLICS* in the urban industrial areas with residual loyalty to the Democratic Party but growing animosity to liberal measures such as busing, expanded welfare, "soft" foreign policy and social engineering. This substantial fragment of the Catholic bloc is in transition, fast becoming blue-collar bourgeoisie but still susceptible in large numbers to the magic of the Kennedy name.

• *CATHOLIC TRADITIONALISTS AND MILITANTS* whose political perspective is strongly influenced by religious issues—especially abortion. This group draws its strength from every geographical and economic level. When activated by well-organized "Right to Life" crusaders and other one-issue militants, it can have a disproportionately strong impact in low-turnout primaries and local contests. Ironically, this Catholic bloc is potentially anti-Kennedy because of his weak stand on abortion and his opposition to school prayer.

• *"ASSIMILATED" CATHOLICS,* mainly middle- and upper middle-class small businessmen, professionals and their families who, like most Americans in the same socio-economic bracket, are increasingly humanist in outlook and unlikely to think of themselves or the candidates in terms of religious labels. In effect, they have ceased to be Catholic as far as voting is concerned.

• *HISPANIC CATHOLICS* are still strongly religious and, in heavily Cuban Miami, heavily Mexican-American sections of the Southwest, and heavily Puerto Rican areas in the urban Northeast, represent a potential voting bloc, currently diluted by low registration and voter turnout. Even within this category, however, there are several subgroups. The Cubans, mostly refugees from Castro or their children, are comparatively affluent, middle class and militantly anticommunist. They are not monolithically Democratic. The Puerto Ricans are more of a relic of the old Roosevelt coalition, still reliant on Democratic machine politics and patronage and with a large welfare population, especially in New York and New Jersey. The Mexican-Americans fall somewhere in between—comparatively low on the economic ladder but upwardly mobile and located in the Sunbelt, an economic growth area. Though they lean to the Democrats, neither party has them locked up as a bloc.

The same case can be made for the labor vote. Union leadership—and the ample financial and technical assistance it commands—is still at the disposal of the Democratic Party. But what about labor votes? Thanks in large part to the past victories of the union movement, today's teamster, construction worker or skilled machinist often has a house in the suburbs, kids in college, and an essentially middle-class lifestyle. He voted to protect his interests twenty years ago and he does the same thing today. But his interests are different. In 1980 he is more worried about inflation, fuel prices, taxes and crime than he is interested in extending the welfare state. This doesn't make him an automatic Republican voter by any means, but it does mean that candidates of both parties who want his vote must appeal to him more as a respectable burgher with a vested interest in the *status quo* than as a struggling member of the proletariat.

The people, say the pollsters, cry out for leadership—and after more than a decade of war, scandal, economic disruption and mediocre leadership, no doubt they do. But what kind of leadership? They want a President who will inspire them rhetorically and excite them without calling on them to make serious material sacrifices. But most of all they want a President who will help them to hold onto the essentially middle-class, consumer status they have worked hard to achieve and now feel in danger of losing.

Their motto is, "To have and to hold," and the party whose nominee convinces them that he will help them to do this will win the White House in 1980.

Having concluded this, and having spent more time than most of us would prefer wandering through the political obstacle course that still awaits the candidates of 1980, let us, in the words of Sir Winston Churchill, "pass with relief from the tossing sea of Cause and Theory to the firm ground of Result and Fact"—the candidates themselves.

PART II

The Democrats

The Democratic Party will live and continue to receive the support of the majority of Americans just so long as it remains a liberal party.
—*Franklin Delano Roosevelt*

I never said all Democrats were saloonkeepers; what I said was all saloonkeepers were Democrats.
—*Horace Greeley*

Today's Democratic Party still bears traces of both the Roosevelt and Greeley descriptions. The New Deal coalition, while not the thriving political organism it once was, survives as a kind of crumbling but teeming tenement, still crowded but liable to be torn down at any moment. And as Greeley put it in his half-jesting way, the Democrats are still the sloppy, sudsy, largesse-dispensing "party of the people" in the estimation of millions of Americans, mostly friendly but, in growing numbers, dubious. It has lost its grip on many of its members who, while nominally still Democrats, tend more and more to cross over or split their votes at the national level.

But the Democratic Party remains by far the largest organized political entity in America, and the oldest, biggest and most successful party of its kind in the history of democracy with a small "d". Nevertheless, all three of the serious candidates for the 1980 Democratic nomination—including incumbent President Jimmy Carter—are not only running, but running away from *much of their party's traditional image as a big-hearted, small-brained charity operation. Seeking the party's embrace, they simultaneously flee from its perjorative labels ("bleeding heart," "do-gooder" and even the once-respectable "lib-*

eral"). This has caused much dismay among old-line progressives, trade unionists and closet socialists who, since the days of Roosevelt, have considered the Democratic Party the nearest thing to a socialist party attainable in the United States. But they, unlike rank-and-file voters, have nowhere else to go.

It's hard to think of three more starkly contrasting men than Jimmy Carter, Teddy Kennedy and Jerry Brown; politics has always made for even stranger sparring partners than bedfellows. Carter, the dogged incumbent with his odd mix of idealism, piety and petty-mindedness, sometimes politically cunning and sometimes politically inept, is still either a riddle or a disappointment to most of the electorate, including many of the people who voted for him in 1976. Kennedy, with that obviously sincere sense of family tragedy and destiny that is so hard to square with his own flawed personality and often irresponsible, self-indulgent lifestyle, is a man who has achieved fame and popularity without, so far, having had to face real executive responsibilities. He is the candidate with both the strongest single asset, the sentimental mantle of Camelot, and the strongest single liability, the "sleeper" issue of personal fitness. Jerry Brown, the maverick dark horse from California, has both a sharp, lucid side and a streak of the crank mystic about him. He could be a harbinger of future politics or just the latest sociopolitical novelty item to be cast up by California.

In the pages that follow, I have tried to individually portray each man as he is, or at least as he seems to be on the basis of the best available evidence and the most plausible insights into it. I have tried to weigh both their fitness and their chances for nomination. As men, all *three are more colorful—not to say more bizarre—than their Republican equivalents. And the most colorful of the Republicans, John Connally, is an ex-Democrat. For this reason, the Democrats' contest is more likely to be an intensely personal one. For "personal," please read "dirty" if you happen to be a political cynic.*

But then bitter intraparty rough-housing has always been meat and drink to the Democrats, who pride themselves on their lustiness in battle and who sometimes really seem to draw strength from the exhilaration of a good, knockdown nomination brawl. The reason, I would suggest, is that, unlike the average Republican politico, the bulk of involved Democrats actually enjoy *politics at the hand-to-hand combat level, a taste that has sometimes been their making and sometimes, as in 1968 and 1972, their undoing. Help or hindrance, there will probably be even more mayhem than usual on the road to their 1980 convention.*

1. JIMMY CARTER: The Incredible Shrinking President

. . . and this time it vanished quite slowly,
beginning with the end of the tail, and
ending with the grin, which remained some
time after the rest of it had gone.
—Lewis Carroll's description of
the Cheshire Cat, Alice in Wonderland

SCOFF IF YOU like, O unbelievers, but to date the most prescient piece of journalism to appear about Jimmy Carter was published, not in the hallowed pages of the *New York Times* or the *Washington Post,* but on page 23 of the September 4, 1979 issue of *Midnight/Globe,* one of the nation's tattier tabloids. There, in bold black and white (or rather in smudged black and dingy, off-yellow news pulp), stood a small but striking piece of the future revealed. One Marge Mann, identified by the editors as "a famous Los Angeles psychic" whose "reputation is fast becoming known throughout the world," informed those who would but heed her that "Jimmy Carter will suffer from exhaustion and be forced to slow down his pace."

A mere eleven days later, a moaning, gray-faced President Carter was dragged—too weak to kick or scream—off the course of a 6.2 mile amateur jogging marathon in the hills of Maryland, a few hundred yards from the presidential retreat at Camp David. Ms. Mann's prediction having become fact, more respectable members of the media quickly grabbed the story and, to continue the metaphor, ran with it. Mr. Colman McCarthy, a talented (for a nonsmoking, teetotalling vegetarian) essayist with the *Washington Post* happened to be not only on the scene, but running in the race himself as entry number 752. At the time of the presidential collapse, he was within eye and earshot of the foundering first executive.

"I heard a series of groans," McCarthy would recount. "They were not the usual pants and grunts of breathlessness that are the common sounds of runners as they battle gravity and themselves. I looked to my left, and suddenly the president began to stagger. His face was ashen. His mouth hung open, and his eyes had an unfocused look."

What followed was predictable enough. Two Secret Service men grabbed Carter under each arm and propped him up. As far as this race was concerned, he was finished. And everyone seemed to know it but Jimmy Carter, who lurched forward, mumbling that "he wanted to keep going." Still protesting feebly, he was dragged off by his worried guardians, only to show up a few hours later, hosed down and in fresh clothing, at the finish line. Having arrived by motor, he was capable of exclaiming: "I feel great!"

It was a scene rich in possible interpretations. Symbolic of the greater race to come? A typical example of an ambitious but inadequate loser biting off more than he could chew? A stirring case of pluckiness in adversity? A cheap publicity stunt that backfired? Or one more sad, small glimpse into the heart and mind of a chronic overachiever? Maybe it was a bit of all five. Whatever else it was, it had a lingering aroma of the fishy about it. For some weeks the Carter White House had been boasting to the press that their man had already clocked an average jogging speed of 7 minutes 30 seconds to the mile.

Quite aside from the collapse, Carter never managed to do better than 8 minutes 25 seconds in this, his first publicly-timed run. Had Jimmy Carter been fibbing about his jogging prowess? Or had he himself been the willing victim of sycophantic in-house timekeepers? Either way, shouldn't he have known better?

Instant analysis, as usual, was not wanting. Dr. Theodore Cole, chairman of the department of physical medicine and rehabilitation at the University of Michigan, informed reporters by long-distance that "psychological stress" could have been the cause of the presidential pooping out. But Dr. Cole hastened to add that for a runner as accomplished as Mr. Carter claimed to be, "it would be uncommon to drop out that soon." Dr. Vernon B. Mountcastle, chairman of the division of physiology at Johns Hopkins Medical School, was a bit more direct. These things happen, he said, when "one tries to run farther than one is used to. . . ."

This, as many of his critics have long insisted, is exactly what Jimmy Carter has been trying to do for most of his political life. Gimmickery, often successful but latterly falling rather flat, has always been a Carter hallmark. One reason he is perceived by so many Americans today as a weak leader is because he has always cultivated ambiguity (or really had few thought-out beliefs) and has tried to win popularity through shallow gestures: wearing a sweater to help solve the energy shortage; taking a trip on a riverboat to keep the country calm during a Cuban minicrisis; urging everyone to say something good about America to rescue the nation from spiritual malaise; and shifting wardrobes, hairdos or cabinet members when his popularity plunges sharply.

What is disturbing about this is not that it is opportunistic, but that Carter probably really believes that these *are* solutions—that there is no deeper vision of leadership beneath the surface gesture and the cosmetic adjustments. Something is missing, despite the oft-repeated moralisms and the claim to being a thinker immersed in philosophies and systems.

The same missing dimension is evident in many Carter appointees. One of the brightest exceptions, Treasury Secretary Michael Blumenthal, was one of the first to go—despite the fact that he had won the respect of Congress and foreign finance ministers. Blumenthal was considered too independent, too popular, and, most of all, incompatible with White House Chief of Staff Hamilton Jordan, who shares so few of Blumenthal's positive attributes.

Jordan, who is an able man on the campaign trail, has shown no equivalent talent for running the White House. And he hasn't been the only washout. Dr. Peter "Happy Pill" Bourne, who resigned after he was caught faking prescriptions of mood altering drugs for other White House Staffers; Bert Lance (the President's "best friend") who left under a cloud when his tangled and dubious financial practices came to light; and Andrew Young, who was finally sacked after repeatedly embarrassing the United States and using his post as Ambassador to the United Nations as a platform for propagating his own extremist views on foreign policy—all were members of Carter's "Georgia Mafia," personal friends of little national standing or experience whom he brought with him to the White House, rather than risk being eclipsed by a supporting cast of superior stature.

But, again, was this a conscious decision, or was Carter incapable of telling the difference between first rate and second rate? Consider foreign policy. Whatever one may think of Henry Kissinger's ego and his method of ending the Vietnam War, there is no question about his intelligence, effectiveness and the respect he won from foreign powers. Today in his place sit two men whom few dislike and even fewer take seriously, Secretary of State Cyrus Vance and National Security Council Director Zbigniew Brzezinski. Meanwhile, chaos reigns in Iran, the Russians continue to build up their military superiority, the economy wobbles, and friendly foreign powers view American leadership with a mixture of horror, puzzle-ment and suppressed laughter (IS CARTER CONTAGIOUS? was a lead headline in a recent issue of the *Economist,* one of Britain's most moderate, prestigious weeklies).

In less dangerous times, without energy problems, economic uncertainty, genocide in Southeast Asia and Cuban-backed insurrection in many parts of Latin America, it all might be amusing. Not now. And the worst of it is that much of what has happened—some of the most dismal parts of Carter's perform-ance in office—was not only predictable but predicted. Con-sider the following, a short essay that was published in the summer of 1976, when Jimmy Carter was fresh from his nomi-nation victory in New York and still locked in mortal combat with Jerry Ford for the Presidency:

All of my friends say they're afraid Jimmy Carter is just another phony; what worries me is that he's probably to-tally sincere. Then, too, for a history buff like myself there is something hauntingly familiar about the Carter tone, pretensions, and even the accompanying grin. All too often, today's bold new journey is only a rehash of yester-day's bad trip and, curiously enough, the previous owner of the Carter grin and aura also had his professional start in Georgia, although that was way back in 1882 in an Atlanta law office. He, too, was a middle-class son of the South with a rigorous religious upbringing and, after head-ing north, he served one little-noted term as governor before coming out of nowhere to capture the Democratic nomination and, ultimately, the White House. Like Gov-ernor Carter, he read the Good Book every day and never tired of reminding everyone of how godly he was, though unfortunately this led him to the sin of pride and the delusion that all those who opposed him were not merely mistaken, but downright immoral—after all, they refused to recognize his personal mandate from Heaven, didn't they?

The previous owner of the Carter smile promised to bring a new morality and candor to the debauched political process although his own campaign utterances were almost as remarkable for their vagueness as for their high moral tone. In actuality, he raised nothing but expectations, and those so unrealistically that they, his reputation, and general public respect for politics were cruelly dashed in the aftermath.

"Old Horseface," as Washington kids of my father's generation nicknamed him, had been a great candidate and a pathetic President. By the time he left office, a broken man, his Fourteen Points were no more than a stale joke (even God only required Ten Commandments, the French statesman Georges Clemenceau had remarked with a shrug) and his pet project, the League of Nations, was a moribund farce. All that remained of his political legacy was the Federal Income Tax and the pious insanity of Prohibition—that and the lingering memory of a toothy grin that still stares out from many photographs and editorial cartoons of the period. Quick, somebody, call the Exorcist; Jimmy Carter has been possessed by Woodrow Wilson's grin!

And the similarity doesn't end with the deathmask tightness and intensity of the wall-to-wall grimace, either. The same curious mixture of outspoken morality and underlying egotism that doomed Woodrow Wilson to failure as a President is already writ large on what there is of a Carter record. . . .

Perhaps in this naive yet jaded era of shallow imagery and flash impression, people really do hunger for a charismatic Plastic Jesus with soothing personality and platitudes who glosses over the substantive commitments and principles that force voters to think and candidates to stand for something more than real or imaginary inner glow.

So far the Carter strategy has worked remarkably well and my own bet is that he will be very hard to beat in the

[1976] general election . . . and only then, when it may be too late, will we find out all we wanted to know about Jimmy Carter but were afraid to ask. Now don't get me wrong. I've already said that I don't think Governor Carter is a fake. I think he's sincere in the worst sort of way; I think he really *believes* that he is morally superior to the other hounds in the political pack even though his conduct as a candidate has been no more honest, candid, or uplifting than the rest.

It is precisely the genuine self-righteousness of the man that gives me the creeps. Historically, it has been the zealots, not the gasbags and the fixers, who have been the biggest disasters, whether in the case of . . . Woodrow Wilson leading Americans into a hollow holy war that ultimately made the world safe for nothing but hypocrisy, or Jimmy Carter exploiting voter ennui and disenchantment by wrapping himself in a cloak of sanctimony and promising that, if we'll just shut our eyes and follow him, he'll lead us all to a great Cornpone Camelot in the sky . . .[1]

The irony about the Carter appeal to vague ideals as a nonincumbent outsider in 1976 is that, this year, the same ploy is being used against Carter the incumbent by Teddy Kennedy. And Teddy can offer the voters a more authentic, cornpone-free variety of the Camelot dream. Apologies for quoting this rather farseeing essay at length, but it is important to demonstrate that, for those who looked at the evidence and the indicators closely months before the 1976 elections, it was already possible to predict both Carter's successful election pitch and his future shortcomings as President. Besides, since I'm the one who write the essay, I thought it a simple means of establishing my credentials as a tested political meteorologist.

Carter's tragic flaw as a leader—perhaps unfortunate would

[1]"Old Horseface, Arrogance, and Jimmy Carter" by Aram Bakshian, Jr., *The Alternative: An American Spectator,* page 21, August 1976.

be an adjective more in keeping with his stature—is that he has consistently overestimated the intrinsic power and prestige of *being* President, i.e. of merely occupying the office, and has simultaneously failed to master the dynamics of mobilizing and deploying them. Why? The answer may lie in his basic conception (or lack of any basic conception) of power, leadership and the march of history. I am the last fellow on earth to take psychohistory and amateur analysis seriously. I still find myself convulsed with laughter whenever I reread James D. Barber's pretentious 1977 opus, *The Presidential Character: Predicting Performance in the White House.* Having created an elaborate system of psychological types for Presidents of the past, the venerable Barber then brought his fragile theoretical apparatus to bear on the future, designating Jimmy Carter an "active-positive" president and fondly asserting:

> I believe he will turn out to be a pleasured President, finding, as did FDR and HST and JFK, that life in the Oval Office can be fun—is on the average. . . .

If Carter will have a problem, Barber predicted in 1977 with rather touching absurdity in hindsight, it will be that:

> Like the other active-positive Presidents, his character-based troubles are going to spring from an excess of an active-positive virtue: the thirst for results. . . .

First character-reader Barber gives us his view of the "good" first executive as one who views the Presidency as a sort of adult playpen, and then he warns us that Jimmy Carter's only problem in office will be that he'll be too much of a good thing, a leader with his plate heaped too high with "results"—the very thing the Carter Administration has been sadly lacking in.

Let us therefore discard complicated psychological rating systems such as poor Barber's for some elementary insights based on observed phenomena and matters of record. Take, for instance, the almost obsessive way in which Jimmy Carter tells anyone who will listen about how deeply moved he was when he read Leo Tolstoi's monumental historical novel, *War and Peace.* It's a fair and common-sense maxim that the fewer books a man reads, the more impact those few books that do make it up his mental rapids will have. For Carter, whose literary groundings, to judge from his writing, speeches and conversation, are rather shallow, *War and Peace* seems to have come as a road to Damascus experience, a revelation.

While I am all for broadening the cultural horizons of the denizens of Plains, Georgia, I'm also a staunch believer in the ancient warning that a little knowledge is a dangerous thing. Given the lack of counterbalancing historical reading and insight, Jimmy Carter couldn't have chosen a worse classic than *War and Peace* to open his eyes to the meaning of history and leadership. As most readers will recall, *War and Peace* is set in early nineteenth-century Russia, much of the critical action taking place during Napoleon's disastrous 1812 invasion. Napoleon was defeated; he retreated and lost most of his *Grande Armée* because he overestimated his own strength, underestimated Russia's ability to fight, and failed to calculate the effect of a bad Russian winter. Not to mince words, he did a number of stupid things and he lost. On the other hand Kutusov, the Russian commander, was cautiously cunning, drawing Napoleon on, never risking a decisive battle that could completely destroy his own forces, and making clever use of partisan warfare and the scorched earth policy. In other words, Kutusov did a number of smart things and he won. He provided better thought-out and better-executed leadership, and the result was one of the great turning points in western history.

But Leo Tolstoi didn't see it that way. Tolstoi, who died a Christian mystic and was already heading in that direction when he wrote *War and Peace,* took the view that men do not shape or even significantly modify events. He negated the very idea of positive leadership by concluding that we are all pawns in the hand of a God-directed universal destiny. Thus, when the impressionable Jimmy Carter reached Chapter 1, Part IX of *War and Peace,* he would have read the following passage:

> In historical events great men—so called—are but labels that serve to give a name to an event, and like labels, they have the least possible connection with the event itself. Every action of theirs, that seems to them an act of their own free will, is in an historical sense not free at all, but in bondage to the whole course of previous history and predestined from all eternity.

This is a potentially dangerous view of the world for a leader in a powerful position—especially one with little or no economic or foreign policy experience and with few clear ideas of his own on how to govern, how to lead. And if the same man is convinced that he, as a true believer, is on the best of terms with God, he is encouraged to expect that, as long as he says his prayers and keeps up appearances, the Lord will do the rest, using him as His chosen vessel. In such a case, the nominal "leader" *ceases* to be a leader in the active sense, unless he convinces himself that he has been beamed a special assignment from the Almighty—a part of the preordained master plan. Which is how we get the Ayatollah Khomeinis of this world.

Just as dangerous in a passive way is the other choice open to a leader with Tolstoi's view of the world—sitting and waiting for destiny to drop good or bad developments into one's lap, occupying oneself with humdrum routine and trying to smile through it all since everything important is in the hands of the celestial higher management.

Faced with runaway inflation and the threat of serious recession at home, anarchy in Iran, Soviet combat troops in Cuba,

Marxist insurrection in Central America, and several rounds of international economic crisis, this is how Carter has usually reacted. The only major exception is his handling of domestic politics. When it comes to votes, Jimmy doesn't leave matters to God; he is one of the most energetic, obsessive campaigners ever to occupy the White House. Perhaps this is because he believes that vote-garnering is too mundane a matter for the Lord to dirty his hands with. Whatever the reason, Jimmy Carter has been off and running for a second term from the moment of his Inaugural in 1977. However, because of his reliance on surface symbolism rather than performance, much of his energy has been wasted. He seems to have trouble distinguishing between running as a challenger and running as an incumbent—the difference between being a "Mr. Clean" outsider crusading against Washington, and being a less than dazzling head of the Washington establishment himself. Only belatedly, and with considerable prodding from the pols and the polls, has Carter begun to grasp the fact that the same people who will vote for a challenger on the basis of vague image often insist on judging an incumbent by his performance.

What shape is the Carter incumbency in? He has had his successes, but they have been conditional or are still pending, most notably the fragile peace initiative in the Middle East. Carter as statesman may have "won" by getting his Panama Canal Treaty through the Senate, but politically handing the Canal over to a hostile Panamanian military strongman was far from popular, especially among the more conservative elements of the Democratic Party—the very group Carter must hold if he is to turn back the Kennedy threat. The SALT II arms-control treaty, whatever its ultimate fate, is not the kind of issue that will rally mass support. And the same is true of necessary but unglamorous or unpopular energy policies such as deregulation of domestic oil prices. More important than any one of these issues, however, is the overall impression of a President who has never really managed to get his grip. Human nature being what it is, Americans always complain about an Imperial Presidency when they have one, and then bemoan the lack of strong leadership once presidential wings have been clipped. All of these factors must play a part in evaluating Carter's strengths and weaknesses as a candidate for renomination. But how do we do it?

There are as many ways of handicapping candidates as there are political pundits. In applying my own system to Jimmy Carter and the rest of the class of 1980, I make no special claims for it. It is simple—probably too simple for the scholars and the statisticians—and it is definitely arbitrary, subjective and hunch-oriented.

On the other hand, it does seem to work. I have been right about the last four presidential elections and seven of the last eight Democratic and Republican nominees early on in the race (the exception was Carter, whom I didn't spot as a winner until after New Hampshire in 1976). For more detailed, documented calls, I can cite the prediction I made in October of 1975 in the *Boston Globe* that Gerald Ford would beat out Ronald Reagan for the Republican nomination in 1976, but that Reagan would come close to upsetting him, and the result of the intraparty bitterness would seriously handicap Ford's chances in November; likewise my August 1976 analysis (actually written some weeks earlier) predicting Jimmy Carter's strength as a candidate and inadequacy as a potential President.

Anyway, for what it's worth, here's how it's done. I evaluate each major candidate for nomination using seven basic categories, first verbally weighing them and describing their assets and liabilities in each category, and then mathematically scoring them by category. The totals are then compared to rank the candidates (for the charts scoring the candidates, see *Part V: Gentlemen, Place Your Bets!*). In the individual chapters on the candidates, I include the verbal evaluations.

Because this seven-section system is far from scientific, and to avoid any danger of its being taken completely seriously, I call it *Bakshian's Seven Deadly Whims.* Point by point, but with varying scales of importance, the Seven Deadly Whims are:

1. *LEADERSHIP:* Both as perceived by the voters and as actually demonstrated by the candidate's public record.

2. *COMMUNICATION:* The candidate's talent as a self-seller, his advocacy skill as both a formal speaker and an impromptu "talker," debater and performer. This category takes in not only content and delivery but appearance, radio-television potential and the ability to project that annoying but important cliché quality, "charisma."

3. *ORGANIZATION:* The candidate's track record as an organizer and team builder, his ability to choose lieutenants and delegate authority effectively; the calibre of his staff and state and local supporters will have as much or more to do with the day-to-day success of his campaign as the candidate himself.

4. *WAR CHEST:* Can he attract the necessary campaign funds, and can he and his people do a good job of collecting and allocating them? The late Nelson Rockefeller, for example, was usually over-funded, but once he left his familiar turf in New York State, he seldom got value for money in his unsuccessful bids for the GOP nomination.

5. *AGE/HEALTH:* What shape is the candidate in and how much good time does he have left, both in fact (to the extent that this can be determined) and in popular estimation?

6. *MARRIAGE/FAMILY:* Good, bad or indifferent vibes? Would you want to live next door? Can mom and the brats campaign effectively, or at least avoid serious bloopers and contretemps?

7. *WILD CARD:* This can be positive but is usually nega-

tive. Are there skeletons or scandals in the closet? Is there any half-formed cloud of doubt hanging over the candidate's head—be it based on substance or image—that won't go away and could grow? And, if so, how serious is it? On the positive side, does the candidate have any useful surprise tactics or reserve issues he can spring at an opportune moment?

If most of the above points seem to concentrate on the candidate rather than the issues, so, the pollsters tell us, do most of the voters. One should also bear in mind that the candidate's choice of and positioning on key issues are an important part of his leadership evaluation (Whim 1), and his effectiveness as an issues advocate is an important part of his communication skill (Whim 2). Similarly, his handling and choice of issues will be a determining factor in the quality of staff and supporters he attracts (Whim 3), and an even bigger factor in his ability to raise campaign funds from key interest groups (Whim 4).

So, while *Bakshian's Seven Deadly Whims* is only a system in the loosest sense of the word, and far from infallible, it isn't all that whimsical either. As an old White House colleague of mine, *New York Times* columnist and incorrigible punster Bill Safire, might put it, "You whim a few and you lose a few." How about Jimmy Carter?

CARTER LEADERSHIP (Whim 1)

"One of the things that strikes a wandering journalist, his head full of pollsters' statistics about President Carter's political troubles, is that it's hard to find anyone who dislikes Jimmy Carter," says *Wall Street Journal* columnist Vermont Royster. "Even his eager opponents feel it necessary to preface any criticism with 'Mr. Carter is a very nice man . . .' " But Mr. Royster is quick to point out that "likeability" cuts both ways as far as presidential leadership is concerned: "The leader whom 'everybody likes' is spared enemies. He may also be bereft of committed supporters. Who can lead to battle if none do follow?"

This is a big part of Jimmy Carter's leadership problem. Hated by few, nearing the end of his first (and perhaps only) term in office, he is also taken seriously by few as a strong leader, a view, incidentally, that one finds reflected overseas in most allied capitals. Given high marks for integrity and good intentions, Carter has not been able to make the Presidency work for him as a leadership pulpit. One national poll taken late in 1979 by the Associated Press and NBC found that only 6 percent of the public felt that Carter had been "very effective as a leader" while 29 percent found him "not at all effective" and 63 percent gave him an ambivalent "somewhat effective" rating. By contrast, the same national sampling gave Teddy Kennedy a 22 percent "very effective" rating and only 17 percent rated him "not at all effective."

Unlike his rivals for the nomination, however, Carter *is* the President, as Richard Nixon used to constantly remind us (or was it David Fry?). Unique among candidates, Jimmy Carter has the potential for using his executive powers in a dramatic way, especially in reaction to crisis. He *could* salvage his image as a leader at any time between now and the convention, but he could also further tarnish it by mishandling—or seeming to mishandle—problems that other candidates need only talk about.

Leadership *assets* for Carter:

• Perceived as "decent" and well-intentioned.
• Has the power to take real rather than rhetorical action on the issues.

Leadership *liabilities* for Carter:

• Seen as ineffectual and having failed to live up to his campaign promises of leadership.

• Generally has *not* used the powers of the incumbency effectively to solve real problems *or* bolster his own image.

So, on the leadership front, Carter is weak and vulnerable, but not down and out. And he still has the weapon of the incumbency—albeit a risky, double-edged one—at his disposal.

One of the amusing sidelines of the whole leadership question is the bumbling way it is treated by many supposedly serious, insightful members of the media. Given daily or weekly deadlines, and ever hungering for a fresh dramatic slant, they tend to magnify the insignificant, sometimes at the cost of blinding themselves to the truly important. Most of them don't seem to have that clear an idea of what leadership is themselves, much less of how to measure it. Theodore White, a talented narrator with an unfortunate addiction to the melodramatic, has tried to portray presidential leadership as a kind of secular high priesthood—a notion that would have horrified the signers of the Constitution who invented the office, and that would raise a belly laugh from most Presidents in their nonmegalomaniac moments.

Even a thoughtful observer like *Time* magazine's Hugh Sidey goes all gooey inside when writing about the Presidency. Presidents do not think, learn, decide and lead—they undergo "internal metamorphosis"; they are transformed through "alchemy"; and they cause usually rational journalists like Sidey to measure their leadership by such, if I may say so, *whimsical* means as a change in the set of the presidential jaw. Thus, according to Mr. Sidey:

President Carter looks different. Older, gaunter, grayer, tireder. All that is true. But it is something else.

Men and women who have worked with the President have looked up at the man across from them and seen something physically new, beyond the natural changes of aging. They have asked themselves exactly what it is—the intensity in the eyes, or the mouth line, or the fractional shift in his jaw set? No one seems quite sure. It could be as much what he says and how he says it. But from both the White House and beyond there is testimony that he is more of a President.

Perhaps Facial Politics are an inevitable extension of Body Language. Who knows? But the fact that White House staffers and sophisticated journalists like Sidey are reduced to looking for signs of statesmanship in the angle of Jimmy Carter's jaw gives an idea of how desperate people are for any signs of presidential leadership, and a measure of the leadership gap Carter faces in seeking renomination.

CARTER COMMUNICATION (Whim 2)

Communication is the outward manifestation of a candidate's inner content. A good speaker can win admirers for the quality of his technique, but sooner or later he has to say something worth hearing or all of his dramatic gestures and skillfully manipulated pauses and intonations go for naught. As a formal speaker Jimmy Carter has problems—both with content and delivery. His curious cadence, the emphasis on unexpected words in the middle of sentences, and the tendency to grin at inappropriate moments make him difficult to follow; a tendency to drone in monotone loses many listeners after the first few minutes of the typical Carter speech; his rather weak voice, especially in a crowded auditorium, can only make itself heard by turning shrill; and his speechwriters have not, on the whole, given him very good written material to work with.

On the other hand, Jimmy Carter is fairly good as an impromptu speaker, demonstrating a quick mind and, usually, a good control over his emotions—and over the impulse to make wild promises. The exceptions, however, have occasionally been damaging, such as his ad-libbed promise not to tolerate the "status quo" of Soviet combat units in Cuba, followed by an official decision to do just that. Carter is also a reasonably good debater and a man who usually projects a good level of calm and a clear conscience.

Interestingly enough, Teddy Kennedy, Carter's main challenger, is his exact opposite in communications. Teddy is fine with a script, especially one larded with Camelot rhetoric. It's not that Teddy is a great orator; he just *sounds* so much like his two martryed brothers. On the other hand, Teddy tends to fall apart when he has to think on his feet. He has trouble forming complete sentences. Except when briefed in detail, Kennedy rambles, giving the impression of confusion at best, deviousness at worst. He will almost certainly outdo Carter on the stump, delivering prepared copy to live audiences, and in rehearsed, scripted television and radio spots. But Carter holds the edge both as an interviewee and as a debater.

Some of the heaviest criticism of Carter the communicator happens to have come from one of his former speechwriters, James Fallows, currently Washington editor for the *Atlantic Monthly.* As an ex-speechwriter for two Presidents myself, perhaps I took an undue interest in Fallows' critique of Carter. To a certain extent, it reflected Fallows' own lack of understanding—his romantic view of the Presidency as an agency for massive change, and his emotional belief in what he calls "the passionate Presidency." Carter's over-all problem, says Fallows, is that he is a "passionless" President (whatever that means), and that he lacks a well-defined series of priorities and goals—not to mention the ability to follow through and achieve them. Because Jimmy Carter doesn't really understand his job, Fallows seems to be saying, he has failed to make his Presidency stand for anything and, necessarily, has flopped as a communicator for want of anything solid *to* communicate. According to Fallows, the President's first two years in office were "wasted before Carter absorbed what I had thought he knew in the first place."

"Carter often seemed to be more concerned with taking the correct position than with learning how to turn that position into results," Fallows writes in the *Atlantic Monthly*. "Carter did not really know *what* he wanted to do in such crucial areas as taxes, welfare, energy and the reorganization of government."

> In each of these areas, Carter's passionate campaign commitments turned out to be commitments to generalities, not to specific programs or policies. After taking office, he commissioned panels of experts to tell him what to do, usually giving them instructions no more detailed than his repeated exhortation to 'Be bold!'

Little has come of this, beyond an expansion of the federal maze, a substantial increase in the salaries of the White House staff, and the creation of new government agencies and departments, most notably separate departments of energy and education—all actions in direct conflict with his promise to cut back on the cost of government, simplify the bureaucracy and make things run better, like a good engineer.

Carter the communicator, then, is hostage to Carter the leader. The failures of the latter cause or aggravate the failures of the former. Until he *does* better, he really doesn't have that much positive to talk about.

In capsule Carter's Communication *assets* are:

• Comparatively good on his feet, answering questions, debating or interacting with people informally.
• Projects honesty, good intentions, clear conscience and a lack of "political" deviousness.

Carter's communication *liabilities:*

• Mediocre voice, pronounced regional accent, and low quality content and delivery of most formal speeches.
• Larger problem of lacking a cohesive program or set of related, positive achievements to talk about.

Again, part of what is missing in Jimmy Carter's skill as a communicator is what seems to be missing in the man—a strong sense of direction and *applied* principles. As former Carter speechwriter Fallows points out about one of Carter's key campaign issues in 1976:

> When he [Carter] said that, this time, tax reform was going to happen, it was not because he had carefully studied the tales of past failures and learned how to surmount them, but because he had ignored them so totally as to think his approach had never been tried.

And this, in turn, was caused by a "willful ignorance" in Carter himself, explainable, according to Fallows, "only by a combination of arrogance, complacency and—dread thought —insecurity at the core of his mind and soul."

Dread thought indeed. But perhaps Mr. Fallows has gone a bit far. To be sure, Mr. Carter has repeatedly overestimated his ability to cope with events and underestimated the seriousness of the problems (or the value of other people, especially Washington "insiders," to help in solving them). But he seems to have learned at least a part of his lesson. Nowadays, whenever a crisis breaks, the White House is quick to call in old Washington hands like Clark Clifford. And, after using his considerable talents as a trade negotiator and to represent the United States in the delicate Israeli-Egyptian peace talks, he has now tapped former Democratic National Committee Chairman Robert Strauss—the ultimate political insider—to run his campaign for renomination and reelection.

CARTER ORGANIZATION (Whim 3)

The greatest virtue in a prince, if one can believe an epigram of Martial's, is to know his friends. Jimmy Carter's problem is that, with the exception of the very Georgia Mafia that has caused him so much embarrassment, he doesn't have that many trusted political friends, and he knows it. Allies of convenience and enemies of *his* enemies, yes. But deeply, personally committed political friends, no. Carter simply wasn't on the national political scene long enough before becoming President to gather a deep-rooted following of his own, especially among top politicians and political technicians.

Because Teddy Kennedy was not a candidate in 1976, many Kennedy Democrats backed Carter, especially after his nomination had been recognized as a virtual *fait accompli.* After the election, many of them were appointed to important federal posts. Today, although a number have already jumped ship, resigning to declare for Teddy Kennedy, others still remain in key posts throughout the bureaucracy. They represent a fifth column for Kennedy and a potential source of leaks, political sabotage and nervous attrition for Jimmy Carter.

The sprinkling of resignations that followed Teddy Kennedy's decision to run was an embarrassment for Carter and may have had a mildly dampening effect on his supporters' morale. But it's the Kennedy backers who *don't* resign that he really needs to worry about. When a political lame duck like former Iowa Senator Dick Clark (defeated in 1978 because of a liberal voting record that antagonized a majority of Iowans) resigns as Carter's ambassador for refugee affairs, it makes bad headlines for a day or two. But Clark himself is no great loss. In fact he was only given the post in the first place as a favor, after Iowa's voters handed him his walking papers. His desertion of the President who gave him a job when he needed one is not likely to add much luster to the Kennedy camp.

White House sources were quick to react to the Clark resignation by stating that this was only the beginning of "a sorting-out process as Democrats choose up sides." Carter pollster Pat Caddell went even further, summoning up an image from *Gone with the Wind:*

It's just like the days before the war in 1861. Families are getting together for the last time, shaking hands and going off to do bitter battle. People are having to decide their loyalties.

Not quite, but something close to it. For many of the Democratic Party loyalists who helped Carter win in 1976 and then shared in the political spoils and the running of the government, he has never been first choice. More than Hubert Humphrey in 1968, and far more than Lyndon Johnson in 1964, Jimmy Carter, while nominally backed by the political apparatus of the state, cannot trust many of his own troops. Despite Vice President Mondale's warning that intraparty strife could be "so poisonous to the Democratic Party that no Democrat can win" in November, the Kennedy fifth column can be counted on to spring one booby trap after another as the nomination campaign proceeds.

Dirty tricks aside, Carter faces other organizational problems unusual for an incumbent President. Long before there was any question of Kennedy or any other Democrat challenging him, Carter was plagued by staff trouble. Scandal or ineptitude had already forced him to part with many of his most trusted, personally closest White House aides—Dr. Bourne, Bert Lance, Andy Young and Tim Kraft (who was first shifted from the White House to the Carter reelection committee and then, in a third downgrading, was superseded by Robert Strauss). Carter's congressional liaison staff—his vital link to the Democratic majorities in the Senate and the House of Representatives—is probably the most inept of modern times, headed by Frank Moore, a slow-talking, slow-moving member of the Georgia Mafia. While most Democrats in Congress would prefer to avoid a divisive nomination battle, and while a majority of the party's moderates and conservatives still are more at home with Carter than Kennedy, it is less than likely that the Carter White House is capable of making very effective use of their tacit support.

As for the Democratic Party's liberal wing, Carter's main link to it is his well-liked but easy-going Vice President, Fritz Mondale. Like Carter, Mondale is a man nobody hates—and not too many people take seriously as a strong political force. In 1978, in spite of his strenuous campaigning, Mondale could not even hold his native Minnesota for the Democrats. A bastion of liberal strength while Hubert Humphrey was alive, Minnesota now has a Republican governor, two Republican senators and an evenly balanced House delegation.

It says something about the crudeness or naivete of White House chief of staff Hamilton Jordan and other key Carter political advisors that some of them entertained hopes of making Fritz Mondale the chief hatchet man of the campaign—the traditional role assigned to Vice Presidents like Nixon under Eisenhower and, a decade later, Agnew under Nixon. It is one for which the mild-mannered Minnesotan is singularly unfit by temperament and ideology. There *is* a need for such a point-man, and the point he should be making is valid: that Teddy Kennedy's extreme liberalism (to the left of even George McGovern, if one goes by the rating system of Americans for Democratic Action, the arbiter of liberal orthodoxy) is completely out of step with the current public mood. "Now is the time we've got to pin the big-spender, inflationary label on him [Kennedy] before he changes clothes," was the way one Carter aide put it at the outset of the campaign. But Mondale is not the man for the job and, with the exception of Robert Strauss, who will have his hands full behind the scenes, Carter has no popular national party figure in his camp who is really up to the work.

Far from attacking Kennedy, Mondale spends most of his time these days making lame apologies for Carter. "No matter who was President for the past three years," runs a standard Mondale refrain, "he would be having trouble because of the issues he has to deal with. If Kennedy had been President, inflation would be where it is. . . ." What matters, though, is that Kennedy is *not* President and Carter *is*—and, if we are to carry Mondale's reasoning to its logical conclusion, this is not a good time to be an incumbent President. Hardly a strong sales pitch for Jimmy Carter.

Relatively recent White House appointees of stature like Hedley Donovan, former editor-in-chief of *Time* Incorporated Publications, Washington lawyer Lloyd Cutler, and management expert Alonzo McDonald may serve to lessen the staff mess at the White House just as Robert Strauss may be able to shape up the campaign committee. But all of these able, tested political veterans are still subordinate to the man one Washington wag has tagged "the ignoblest Georgian of them all," White House chief of staff Hamilton Jordan. And about Jordan, there *is* a party consensus, perhaps best articulated by Democratic Congressman Andrew Maguire of New Jersey. "It is utterly appalling to many of us," he lamented after Jordan's elevation to chief of staff, "that the White House thinks that the answer to its problems is giving more authority to Hamilton Jordan."

Known to most of the public mainly for his rudeness at diplomatic dinners and his Amaretto-spewing antics in second-rate Washington saloons, Jordan is intensely disliked on Capitol Hill and among state Democratic leaders for his inaccessibility and lack of political sophistication. Still, Carter trusts Jordan and is comfortable with him, their relationship going back to the President's early days as a struggling, obscure Georgia politician; and there are so few others Jimmy Carter really knows or trusts. In fairness to Jordan, for all his crudity and his penchant for making unsavory headlines, he is no fool. He has a rough-hewn but effective instinct for politics and is probably more capable of learning than the man he serves. But he is a horrible administrator, as he himself has admitted more than once. And as far as image goes he is a blot on the Carter

White House of international proportions, as witness the following description of him in the London *Telegraph:*

> [Jordan] has no political philosophy; he is no more than boozily boorish in the gentle way of so many middle-class Southerners afflicted with mild inferiority complexes. . . . It is indeed an awesome thought that such a scruffy, disorganized and even uncouth provincial can have been saddled with so much responsibility.

But there he is, the presiding genius of the Carter White House and the guiding spirit of the Carter campaign—the crass embodiment of Jimmy Carter's staff and organizational problems. Still it was Jordan's masterful grasp of the complicated Democratic Party procedural reforms that saw Carter through to victory in 1976 against nationally more prominent rivals. That counts for something, but in 1976, Carter wasn't running as a weak incumbent, and Teddy Kennedy wasn't running against him.

Organizationally then, Carter comes out somewhere below the middle. He has the advantages of the incumbency, but they are diluted by the Kennedy fifth column in his own Administration and party apparatus, and his comparatively low standing with rank-and-file Democrats. Carter has several good men close to the top—most notably campaign chief Robert Strauss—but the calibre of most of his White House and campaign staffers is markedly inferior to Kennedy's. Carter is on the defensive, and the only way he can take the offensive is by bitterly attacking Teddy Kennedy, something he cannot afford to do directly; yet he has no prestigious surrogate willing to do it for him.

And if luck counts for anything, since 1977 Jimmy Carter has had a consistent record of poor organizational luck—everything from bungling interpreters in Poland to an accident-prone First Lady's staff, which on two separate occasions managed to link Rosalynn Carter to mass murderers (having her send the late Reverend Jim Jones a cordial hand-written note thanking him for sharing his insights into social issues, and providing an autographed photo of the First Lady shaking hands with an Illinois Democratic volunteer by the name of John Wayne Gacey a few months before that worthy was arrested for a long string of homosexual murders).

On that macabre note, let us turn to the rather funereal state of Jimmy Carter's campaign funding.

CARTER WAR CHEST (Whim 4)

By late 1979, the Carter campaign was already in serious financial trouble. The money just wasn't coming in. A "seasonal lull," some Carter loyalists called it, but contributions to Kennedy had already started pouring in before he formally announced his candidacy on November 7th. The Carter committee was even having trouble meeting its own payroll before the campaign had officially begun. Fittingly, one of the first people to defect to the Kennedy camp when it became clear that Teddy had decided to run was Morris Dees, Jimmy Carter's chief fundraiser in 1975, who now signed on as national finance director for Kennedy. Dees' defection took the White House completely by surprise—a further example of poor organization—since he had been working on another fund-raising project for Carter since the summer of 1979.

"A real blow to the President's campaign," was the way one White House aide characterized Dees' switch of sides. "Morris is the guy who kept the campaign afloat during the early primaries [in 1976] when we needed money." Now the man who bailed out the Carter campaign last time around is working for Kennedy, casually pledging to raise "a quick couple of million dollars" for him by New Year's Day, 1980. "I ... still have great respect for Jimmy Carter," Dees explained to a *Los Angeles*

Times correspondent, "but I'm philosophically more comfortable with Senator Kennedy."

And there he put his finger on one of Carter's biggest financial troubles. The largest, most reliable sources for Democratic campaign contributions lie in the liberal wing of the party—trendy figures from television, films and the recording industry who can raise millions at a single rally or rock concert; wealthy but liberally-oriented millionaires (most of their conservative and moderate brethren are Republicans); and of course that bottomless spring of Democratic financial and volunteer support, the trade union movement. None of these groups were ever overly enamored of Jimmy Carter. They backed him against Jerry Ford in 1976 after scattering their support among several more liberal Democratic candidates in the early primaries. Now they have Kennedy to back.

Financially, Carter is not entirely out in the cold. No sitting President with a breath of life in him ever is. Too many vested interests believe in placing starting money on incumbents for practical rather than sentimental reasons, often making matching contributions to rival candidates at the same time. And Carter also has a vast indirect form of campaign funding unique to the incumbent—federal patronage and porkbarrelling. The key here is intelligent, discreet usage. So far, Carter's handling of this *sub rosa* war chest has been clumsy and, in at least one important case, totally wasted. In his futile attempt to win the endorsement of Chicago's fickle lady mayor, Jane Byrne, Carter informally committed himself to $127 million in federal block grants to the Windy City, extended federal funding of 1,300 municipal jobs, Urban Development Action Grants to stimulate $300 million worth of private investment, possible relocation of an Air Force facility at O'Hare International Airport to make way for an expanded commercial terminal, and other federally-funded goodies.

A week later, having welcomed this presidential largesse, Mayor Byrne endorsed Teddy Kennedy anyway. She did not return Carter's engagement gifts. So once again Carter had exercised an asset of incumbency, but in a foolish and counter-productive way.

As Kennedy's lead over Carter began to shrink in the winter polls, and as Robert Strauss and other old pros started making phone calls on Carter's behalf, his war chest woes diminished somewhat. But even though he is President, Jimmy Carter will probably remain the financial underdog in the race for the nomination.

CARTER AGE/HEALTH (Whim 5)

Despite his embarrassing poop-out during the Maryland marathon, Jimmy Carter is in much better physical than fiscal shape. At 55 he remains trim, vigorous and alert, with no history of major illness. His only noteworthy physical problem since entering the White House was more embarrassing than serious. The Presidency, like bookkeeping and bus driving, happens to be a very sedentary calling. In December of 1978, Jimmy Carter, who would later threaten to "whip" Teddy Kennedy's nether regions, was himself visited with a posterior affliction—an attack of hemorrhoids. To his credit, he did not panic in the crisis, although common sense would suggest that he didn't sit it out either. Hindquarters aside, Jimmy Carter seems to have physically borne the burden of the Presidency well. Unless the strain of the office, which so far has confined itself to etching a few extra lines on his face and slightly slackening the executive wattle, knocks him for an unexpected loop, the President should continue to be as fit as or fitter than the rest of the field.

CARTER MARRIAGE/FAMILY (Whim 6)

Al Capp may be dead, but a little bit of Dogpatch lives on in the Carter White House and its adjuncts. Lately, however, things have simmered down. Brother Billy, at first a cuddled novelty and latterly a boozy embarrassment, seems to be doing his best to shut up and sober up; daughter Amy is allowed to pursue her studies in peace and is less often inflicted on state dinner guests and the viewing public; advancing years and stiffening joints have slowed down the volatile Miss Lillian; Chip Carter, once the nearest thing to a gay Lothario in the first family, seems to have buckled down to work as a campaign aide; and the other two Carter offspring, never really at home in the limelight, are avoiding it with a fair amount of success and discretion. Only First Lady Rosalynn, the "Iron Magnolia" of the rictus grin and blazing eye, remains in the foreground, and while she rubs some people the wrong way, she is probably more of an asset than a liability. Washington has never seen anything quite like Rosalynn, who is characterized by some insiders as a much more formidable personality than her husband.

Neither has the White House budget. Mrs. Carter's staff, twenty-one strong, is the largest First Lady's staff in history and costs the taxpayers an estimated $650,000 a year. By comparison, Betty Ford's staff numbered only twelve, with lower salaries and a much smaller budget. Kit Dobelle, Mrs. Carter's "chief of staff," earns the same salary as Zbigniew Brzezinski, in charge of national security, and Hamilton Jordan. Either she's being overpaid or they're being underpaid.

The high cost of the First Lady's staff and activities has created a mini-backlash. "Who elected Rosalynn Carter?" the critics ask. And even within the White House, opinions differ as to her value as a high visibility campaigner. Rosalynn herself is plagued by no such doubts. "I've always said I'm more political than Jimmy," she told one interviewer. "I'm political, he's not. I care what happens. I'll say to him, 'You've got to do this' ... I have influence and I'm aware of it."

Perhaps a little too aware of it, and a little too eager to rattle on about it in the public prints. At least one newsman, *Chicago Tribune* columnist Bob Greene, has pointed up the ironic weakpoint of Mrs. Carter's position as a policy-making First Lady. Rosalynn, he says, should drive all self-respecting feminists up the wall because "she represents that situation that women have justifiably been appalled at: the woman who derives her influence and power solely from her romantic connection with a man." Mrs. Carter, suggests columnist Greene, should be serving tea, not the United States Government.

Point taken, especially if one has ever had to sit through one of Rosalynn's speeches, treacly recitations of the hundred and one ways in which "Jimmah" is the best President the country ever had. Appreciating wifely loyalty is one thing. Having to sit through megadoses of the stuff, delivered in the style of a schoolmarm exhorting a particularly backward group of third graders, is something else.

Unless she's careful, Mrs. Carter, for all of her loyalty, enthusiasm and undoubted sincerity, could prove to be too much of a good thing in her husband's bid for reelection. The time may come when senior aides will have to advise the President (for only he could do it) to releash Rosalynn.

Nevertheless, on balance, Jimmy Carter scores well on Whim 6, *Marriage/Family.* He comes across as a bland, wholesome family man with an intelligent, devoted wife and four fairly run-of-the-mill kids. Neighborly. Comfortable. Noncontroversial. All the things that Teddy Kennedy, as a private citizen, is not.

And now for the last in our litany of whims:

CARTER WILD CARD (Whim 7)

While his main rival has ample reason to beware of scandals, rumors, investigative reporters and things that go bump in the night, Jimmy Carter seems to have little to worry about in the kindred departments of lust and graft. Although Ralph E. Ulmer, the foreman of a federal grand jury investigating alleged links between the Carter White House and fugitive wheeler-dealer Robert Vesco, resigned in protest against what he considered a Justice Department coverup in August of 1979, the commotion soon died down. On October 16th of the same year, the file was officially closed on another source of potential scandal when special federal investigator Paul J. Curran announced that neither President Carter nor his family had violated federal law in their rather unconventional handling of $9 million worth of peanut business passing through the family warehouse in Plains, Georgia.

Conceding that the warehouse business run by first brother Billy Carter had involved a number of irregularities, including "errors" in the records, insufficient collateral and major overdrafts, Mr. Curran still insisted: "Every nickel and every peanut have been traced into and out of the warehouse, and no funds were unlawfully diverted in either direction."

Meanwhile, allegations of cocaine-sniffing by the ever-popular Ham Jordan remained just that—unsubstantiated allegations—the allegers in one case being a dubious set of New York drug peddlers and disco owners under indictment, and, in the other, California Kennedy supporters incapable of offering supporting evidence when pressed to do so. Also forgotten or up in smoke were earlier rumors that members of the Secret Service detail covering one of the Carter sons had complained about familial joint-copping.

And finally, while the snarled financial dealings of Bert Lance, erstwhile "best friend" to the President, continue to attract the interest of the courts, the shadow of Mr. Lance's large, pear-shaped form has receded from the White House and the recollection of most members of the voting public. Unless Jimmy Carter has secretly been lusting after strange women with more than his eyes and his imagination, or some new Carter or senior staff link is found in one of the seemingly closed cases mentioned above, the President should make it through the campaign without a major scandal. On the positive side, he seems equally bereft of wild cards, although as the incumbent there is always the chance that fate will send him an opportune crisis to surmount—something it has failed to provide (at least crises of the *surmountable* variety) so far in his first term.

Such are Jimmy Carter's Seven Deadly Whims, tabulated in chart form, along with those of his rivals, in *Part V.* In summary, the President comes out weak on real and perceived *Leadership,* mixed on *Communication,* vulnerable on *Organization* and *War Chest,* and sound-to-excellent on *Age/Health* and *Marriage/Family.* Barring a mudslinging campaign of the worst sort (or the uncovering of suppressed evidence in seemingly closed cases), he should also be safe from any *Wild Card* scandals, and his past record as a leader incapable of manipulating events means that he will be less likely than most incumbents to use the presidential power effectively to time and mold the headlines to his advantage—all of which balances out to a *Wild Card* low.

As will be seen shortly, compared to Teddy Kennedy's standing in the *Seven Deadly Whims,* Carter comes out marginally weaker, but *only* marginally. He is strong enough to put up a close fight and quite possibly manage an upset. But I will have more to say on that score in *Part V.* For the moment, before we turn to our evaluation of Teddy Kennedy, a final word or two about Jimmy Carter the man. As must already be clear to anyone who has read these pages, I am not much of a Carter fan. In 1976 it seemed to me that, consciously or unconsciously, Jimmy Carter was running under false pretenses—claiming qualifications he did not have and painting an unfair picture of his opponent, Jerry Ford, who in retrospect has proven a more consistently competent (if hardly outstanding) leader than Carter. Once he entered the White House I was also troubled by what seemed to be a Carter obsession with image over substance—or was it his inability to tell the difference between the two? That, and a streak of small-town meanness in Mr. Carter's generally decent character—a grasping, Babbitty ambition that impelled him to keep on running for higher office without really knowing what he would do once he got there.

Yet as the work on this book proceeded, I began to feel something between sympathy and pity for Jimmy Carter as a person. I am convinced that he is one of those people who always fools himself before he tries to fool others; I am convinced that he really does believe in his moral superiority to most of his political foes; and I am convinced that the poor man actually thinks that he has done as good a job or better in the White House than anyone else could have done in his place.

If I am right, then Jimmy Carter holds the Guinness record as the highest-ranking living example of the Peter Principle—and he is a fit object for compassion. Fairly or unfairly, Carter fought hard to win the Presidency in 1976, and he is fighting hard to hold on to it. He has achieved his fondest dream and doesn't want to let go. But along the way he has fallen victim to one of those caprices fate dispenses with such delicious malice—a prank of the sort Nobel Laureate Isaac Bashevis Singer described in the opening lines of his short story *Alone:*

> Many times in the past I have wished the impossible to happen—and then it happened. But though my wish came true, it was in such a topsy-turvy way that it appeared the Hidden Powers were trying to show me I didn't understand my own needs.

One could do worse for an epitaph on Jimmy Carter the politician and, for that matter, the confused popular mood in 1976 which swept him into the White House.

2. TEDDY KENNEDY: Uneasy Runner

*When we are planning for posterity,
we ought to remember that virtue is not
hereditary.*
　　　　　　　　—*Tom Paine,* Common Sense

FOUR YEARS AGO, during a semester spent lecturing at Harvard, I was one of the guests at the annual dinner for the trustees of the Kennedy Institute of Politics. It was one of those odd evenings that only Cambridge and Camelot working together can produce—equal parts glitter and cobweb. The ghosts walked that night. Disembodied spirits from JFK's "Thousand Days," they seemed to have rematerialized from another age, so much had happened in the twelve years since the tragedy at Dallas had destroyed a President and created a myth. Robert McNamara, his hair a bit thinner but still plastered back in the old familiar patent-leather style, was there, his devastated eyes peering out from behind the thin-rimmed spectacles he had worn as JFK's Secretary of Defense, a tight, nervous grin playing across his lips. Lord Harlech, a bit frayed around the edges but still the polished British aristocrat who had shone as ambassador to Washington during the Kennedy years, was on hand to represent the international branch of Camelot, And dozens of lesser luminaries from the old days filled the dining room—half-forgotten faces from a half-forgotten epoch.

Two guests stood out in the ghostly crowd. All eyes were drawn to Jacqueline Onassis and to Teddy Kennedy, the last of the brothers. Mrs. Onassis showed few signs of wear. Beautiful by candlelight and, for that evening at any rate, a charming and animated dinner companion, Jackie was every bit as magnetic and feminine as one had remembered her from a dozen years before. We happened to share a table, and during the course of the evening, we also shared a number of anecdotes and more than a little laughter, much of it at the expense of hack Boston politicians (Mrs. Onassis was raised as a Republican and never quite took to some of her first husband's seamier political cronies). Later the conversation somehow wandered to India, and Jackie joined in a competition for the best imitation of the late Jawaharlal Nehru, whose unintentionally oozing parody of upper-class English mannerisms had amused her no end when she had toured the Subcontinent as First Lady in the early 1960s. From beginning to end, Mrs. Onassis was relaxed, gracious and herself, not straining for effect or playing the role of solemn keeper of the flame. Almost unique in that crowd of walking wounded, she seemed completely alive, a whole person who, whatever her foibles, had lived through the mythic days of triumph and tragedy without being consumed by them. Perhaps, as Mae West once put it, goodness had nothing to do with it. But there was a healthy strength there, and it made her the most pleasant dinner companion in the room.

Teddy was different. He seemed little more than a carelessly assembled collection of spare Kennedy parts—the familiar voice, accent, mannerisms and fragments of Camelot rhetoric, all weak echoes of his dead brothers. Only the eyes were his own and they seemed cold, opaque and very small-set in his ruddy, slightly swollen face (Teddy has since cut his bulk down to about 200 pounds by rigorous precampaign dieting, but in those days, when it seemed that Chappaquiddick had dashed his presidential chances forever, he gave free play to his appetite for thick steaks drenched in Worcestershire sauce, extra helpings of ice cream and other heavy-duty gnoshes). The senatorial jowl and midriff have both been taken in a few notches since then, and what was uncomfortably close to a waddle has once again become a manly stride, but Teddy's eyes haven't changed all that much. They are the eyes of a man alone.

Later that evening a slightly tipsy classicist who happened to wander in from another part of the Faculty Club nudged me with his elbow and nodding in Kennedy's direction muttered, "Observe an unhappy example of the *genus pagarus.*"

I'm not much of a Latin scholar, and this cryptic message, carried to me on the wings of a particularly lethal brandy breath, didn't quite register. My expression must have betrayed me, because my new neighbor quickly added, "*Genus pagarus*—the hermit crab, you dolt!" and then puffed off in quest of another snifter of cognac, leaving me as baffled as before. What on earth had the old boy been talking about?

Four years later, listening to Teddy Kennedy announce his candidacy for the Presidency in a speech that could just as easily have been written for either of his brothers, it finally dawned on me what my boozy friend had meant. The hermit crab, for those readers with as shaky a grounding in natural history as my own, is a "marine decapod crustacean" with a soft, shapeless body that he protects by hiding in abandoned shells that once belonged to better-endowed, departed crustacean relatives. Depending on how you look at it, the hermit crab is either unfortunate or an opportunist, a formless creature who only takes shape by squeezing himself into someone else's empty husk. It can't be very pleasant.

Time magazine has called Teddy the "last of the Kennedy

brothers, the youngest, the most vulnerable, the most thoroughly political." Liberal journalist Robert Sherrill, in the preface to his 1976 book on Teddy, *The Last Kennedy,* went a step further: "A definitive study of Kennedy would be pretty boring," Sherrill wrote. "He is not personally interesting, and no amount of two-paragraph stories about his bar hopping in Georgetown or threading homeward through 4 P.M. traffic at 80 mph can make him so. Nor is he professionally exciting. Like most front-page politicians, he basically serves as the instrument of an efficient staff. He . . . would be eminently forgettable if it were not for tragedy. . . ."

Teddy is important because he is a Kennedy, not because he is Teddy—in *spite* of the fact that he is Teddy, if some of his critics can be believed. He is as much a prisoner of the family legend as the chanting, emotional movie-fan crowds that turn out to greet him wherever he campaigns. His popularity, says West Coast pollster Mervin Field, "is an accumulated, generational perception. He is part of American culture." Which makes him at once something more and something less than a distinct, individual candidate in his own right and own image. "No matter," comments *Time* magazine,

> that John Kennedy blundered into the Bay of Pigs and first widened the war in Viet Nam and saw almost none of his main legislative proposals pass Congress. Americans have a sense, says Theodore H. White, the chronicler of Presidents, 'that Jack Kennedy's Administration was the last one in which it seemed that politics could give people control of their destiny.'

"Why Teddy?" asked the lead editorial in the November 10, 1979 issue of London's *Economist,* its editors apparently immune to the lure of Camelot:

You have to be 35 years old or more and born an American citizen in order to be president of the United States. So why, it may be asked, when some 95 m[illion] people meet these constitutional requirements, should so many Americans now be turning to a man who persuaded someone else to sit his Spanish exam at Harvard, who went on to win a reputation for womanising and hard drinking, and whose behaviour at Chappaquiddick in 1969, when Mary Jo Kopechne died in his car, was, in his own words, indefensible and inexcusable?

The question is not posed simply to denigrate Senator Edward Kennedy, who formally announced on Wednesday that he would seek the Democratic nomination for the presidency next year. All the bad things mentioned above, strung unkindly together in one breath, happened more than 10 years ago. Yet, apart from the fact that Teddy is the brother of Jack and Bobby, they are the things best known about the youngest Kennedy brother, at any rate in Europe. And, at any rate in Europe, where admiration for the elder Kennedys remains high, the question 'Why Teddy?' is persistently asked with genuine bewilderment.

The *Economist* goes on to answer its own question, explaining that one way to win the White House in a modern campaign is for the candidate to have "such an aura of glamour that nobody—voter, journalist or broadcaster—can ignore him; in a country with no official royal family, at a time when political giants are in short supply, few fit that bill better than Teddy Kennedy."

But the undeniable assets that the *Economist* described are only a starting point—or head start—toward the nomination. They are not a guarantee of winning it. The key question about Teddy as a candidate is whether or not the man inside the Camelot shell has what it takes to parlay this built-in lead to victory. What are his individual strengths and weaknesses as a candidate and, when combined with the inherited Kennedy mystique, do they add up to success?

While Teddy owes his fame and position to his family, he also has a record of his own as a three-term senator who has been active and outspoken on a number of issues, and as a controversial celebrity who has made more than his share of gamey personal headlines. "Teddy's career is marked by redundant demonstrations of character weakness," writes "Cato," the Washington columnist for *National Review:*

> Chappaquiddick and college cheating are only part of the problem. For several years in the early Seventies Kennedy conducted himself irresponsibly, as if he never expected to run for national office. He was photographed with other women, wrecked his marriage, and misbehaved in semi-public situations. Just as important, Kennedy's career in the Senate, once promising and always overpraised, has petered out. The major bills that now carry his name are media-magnets rather than strong candidates for passage. His tenure as chairman of the Judiciary Committee, a reflection of his Senate seniority, has been oddly unproductive.

Pulitzer-prize winning columnist George Will, writing in the *Washington Post* a few weeks before Kennedy formally announced, commented on the impact that Kennedy's record, rather than his family name, would have once he made his candidacy official:

> Kennedy is hardly unbeatable. Politicians worry about campaigns that 'peak too early.' Kennedy's campaign may peak the instant it becomes official. After that, he will never again be, as he now is to most people, 'A Kennedy.' People will begin to notice his record.
>
> The electorate is not quite so conservative as it sometimes sounds, but Kennedy is much more liberal than he

will try to appear. Against Kennedy, the Republicans have
a grand chance to seize the middle ground.

And not just the Republicans. Already, the Carter White
House has made it clear that it intends to run its man as a
moderate and to depict Teddy as a left-wing extremist. What
happens when people realize that Kennedy's voting record is
more liberal than George McGovern's? a Carter aide recently
asked one Washington newsman. And another of the President's apparatchiks was quoted in *Time* as saying that Teddy
is "going to get clawed. He's going to bleed, and then he's
going to start dropping in the polls."

And sure enough, as soon as he had announced, Kennedy did
start slipping in some, though not all, of the polls. Even in the
worst of them, however, he maintained a strong lead over
Carter for the nomination and easily beat all major Republican
contenders in head-on samplings. Although Carterites have
branded Kennedy an extremist, and Kennedy has accused
Carter of being the "most conservative Democratic President
since Grover Cleveland," the two rivals are not that different
when it comes to applied policies. They have disagreed on
relatively few of the major issues facing the White House and
the Senate since Carter was sworn in in 1977. In Carter's first
two years in office, Kennedy was one of his strongest backers
in the Senate, and in the first nine months of 1979 he voted
with the Administration fifty-eight times and against it only
ten times.

There have, of course, been important disagreements, most
of them in the field of defense spending or social welfare.
Carter, for example, favored lifting the Turkish arms embargo
and selling jet fighters to Israel, Saudi Arabia and Egypt, both
measures Kennedy voted against. He also pushed decontrol of
natural gas prices and cuts in funding for subsidized housing
programs and subsidized school milk for children above the
poverty line, all opposed by Kennedy. Kennedy backed in-

creased price supports for wheat, a $100 million boost in educational aid to the poor and increased grants to medical students, all of which Carter opposed. But none of these disagreements in themselves are the stuff of which a great national debate is likely to be made. One legislative issue on which they differ, and which could play a key role in low-turnout primary states with a substantial Catholic population, is abortion. Carter opposed providing federal funds for abortions; Kennedy favored it. This could mean strong hostility to Kennedy among Catholic "right-to-lifers" who might otherwise tend to be pro-Kennedy.

But far more controversial than most of his roll-call votes have been some of Teddy's unpassed bills—drastic measures which have never made it out of committee but which, if he were President, would be on the top of Kennedy's legislative agenda. Heading the list is his proposed compulsory national health plan, which he has actively pushed (though with little result in the Congress) since 1972. In its original form, Kennedy's health care plan would have cost $130 billion a year and would have excluded all private sector insurers from participation. Efforts to compromise on cost and allow for private sector participation broke down when the Carter Administration, in July of 1978, demanded further concessions from Kennedy in return for White House backing. Teddy has also introduced major antibusiness measures, most notably legislation to restrict large-scale conglomerate mergers and place a ten-year ban on acquiring new firms with assets of more than $100 million that would cover the nation's sixteen biggest oil firms.

On the other hand, he actively and successfully backed deregulation of airlines. As James M. Perry, the *Wall Street Journal*'s canny political correspondent, sums it up, "the record is surprisingly muddy for a man who has been in the Senate so long. What it really seems to suggest is that the 47-year-old Mr. Kennedy is a politician with strong and traditional liberal views on a number of traditional liberal questions —government spending on social programs, arms control, accommodation with the Soviet Union and restraints on defense spending."

All of these stands would seem to offer sufficient grounds for liberals to support and conservatives and "hawkish" moderates to oppose Kennedy, but as Mr. Perry adds, when Teddy "delves into matters—and he hasn't become deeply involved in many issues—he sometimes is able to depart from his reflexive liberal instincts and arrive at unexpected conclusions," to wit, his efforts to revise and toughen the U.S. Criminal Code and his flirtation with deregulation in some fields.

Despite these occasional forays into moderation, Kennedy's basic voting record is overwhelmingly liberal, as both his most ardent followers and most avid foes agree; Americans for Democratic Action has rated him at a remarkably high 95 percent since 1977 (the very period when he was supposedly beginning to break out of the liberal mold), and the American Conservative Union, the ADA's right wing equivalent, gives him a measly 4 percent rating for his voting record since 1971.

ACU's chairman, Bob Bauman, who also represents Maryland's conservative eastern shore in the Congress, claims that Kennedy "has consistently voted with the radical-left extremists in the Senate." But another, less ideological Republican legislator, Representative Barber Conable of New York, who has served in Congress long enough to have observed all three Kennedy brothers in action, warns that "Ted is the son of Joe Kennedy and the brother of Jack and Bobby. Like them, he accommodates himself to the prevailing views."

If he can pull it off in 1980, Teddy Kennedy will have overcome one of the two biggest barriers between himself and both the nomination and the White House.

The second barrier is scandal—and the whiff of scandal. Chappaquiddick is a large part of it, but it also includes other questions about Teddy's personal behavior, standards and reliability. While there has doubtless been a lot of speculation on this score indulged in strictly to titillate the reading public, in the case of Chappaquiddick at least the issue is a real one because of possible deception, conspiracy and obstruction of justice—not just indiscretion—on the part of Teddy and some of his closest associates. As Robert Sherrill concluded in the introduction to *The Last Kennedy*, his exhaustive book on the subject:

> The Chappaquiddick cover-up was undoubtedly the most brilliant cover-up ever achieved in a nation where investigative procedures are well developed and where the principles of equal justice prevail at least during some of those moments when people are watching. . . . One need not be an admirer of Edward Kennedy to acknowl-edge that he and his attorneys manipulated everything and everyone—federal, state, and local officials, the press, the public, his friends, and events themselves—in a most remarkable way.

Comparing the success of Teddy's Chappaquiddick finessing with Nixon's botching of the attempted Watergate cover-up, Sherrill poses the question, how would Nixon have fared if he had received the same treatment from the authorities and the press that Kennedy did?

What if Nixon's fingerprints had been detected in the Demo-cratic National Committee immediately after the break-in, and he admitted being there but explained that he hadn't realized the office was closed at the time, and was too fatigued to think clearly, which was why he had acted "indefensibly," as he himself described it? What if he then offered to resign if enough voters asked him to, then pleaded guilty to trespassing but not burglary and was given a suspended sentence by a sympathetic judge? What if many of the sordid facts about the case had later been exposed by the media but the judges and prosecuters involved had dismissed the evidence as irrelevant and declared the case closed? If all of this had happened, and congressional committees had been denied access to the White House tapes and been forced to act in secrecy; if Nixon and his senior accomplices in the cover-up had never been forced to undergo rigorous official investigation or cross-examination, and had maintained their political base of support (as Nixon did until well into the *public* hearings, and investigative leaks); then and only then, claims Sherrill, "could our departed President and his partisans boast that he was as clever, and as lucky, as Edward Kennedy."

Mr. Sherrill is not arguing that Richard Nixon got a raw deal. On the contrary, he maintains that he got what was coming to him, whereas Teddy managed to balk justice and receive special treatment every step of the way from the moment his car careened into the water, through an extensive stonewalling operation, to his current promising race for the White House.

Here, as far as they have been established, are the capsule facts of the "tragedy" of Chappaquiddick:

• On July 18, 1969 at approximately midnight, Teddy Kennedy's car plunged off a bridge on Chappaquiddick Island into an eight-foot-deep pond. No report of the accident was made until *after* the police discovered the car the next morning and a diver had extracted the corpse of 28-year-old Mary Jo Kopechne, a Kennedy campaign worker, from the wreck.

• Opinions of those who saw the body differ as to whether Miss Kopechne had been drowned immediately or had suffocated in the air pocket that formed when the car turned upside down as it plunged into the pond. We will never know for sure, because there was no autopsy, although bloodstains were found on the victim's blouse. We do know, however, that if death *was* by suffocation, Miss Kopechne died a slow, agonizing death while Senator Kennedy, allegedly in a state of shock, discussed the accident with two close friends who had attended the barbecue party on the island with himself, three other male guests, Miss Kopechne and five other single girls earlier in the evening—all veterans of family political campaigns.

• Neither Kennedy nor his two friends—his cousin, Joseph Gargan and former U.S. District Attorney Paul Markham (both presumably not in shock, whatever Kennedy's own state may have been)—made any attempt to summon help or inform authorities of the accident. Kennedy then returned to his hotel—and went to bed.

• Only after his car and the body had been discovered by the police the next morning did Kennedy turn himself in, giving Edgartown Police Chief Dominick Arena a partial account of the accident.

• To this day, Mary Jo Kopechne's family complain that they "don't know the whole story" of the events surrounding her death, although they say they think Teddy has "grown up" and they might vote for him in 1980. The parents have also accepted $140,904 in compensation for Mary Jo's death, part of it from insurance coverage, part of it from Teddy Kennedy.

• Markham, Gargan, and the other three male and five female survivors of the party that preceded the accident have never publicly discussed the case; they have effectively stonewalled it.

• Kennedy and company deny that there was any serious drinking at the party. But Jack Crimmins, who sometimes served as Teddy's driver and was an old family errand boy, admitted that he stocked the cottage where the party was to be held with three half-gallons of vodka, four fifths of Scotch, two bottles of rum (he didn't say what size) and two cases of beer. All that was left for him to cart away after the abstemious party was two bottles of vodka, three bottles of Scotch and the beer. It is only fair to assume that someone drank the missing half gallon of vodka, the fifth of Scotch and all of the rum (Teddy, by his own admission, was drinking rum and coke that night).

• The rest is speculation or disputed testimony. For example, one local law enforcement officer, Deputy Sheriff Christopher Look, who was driving home from work on the night of the accident at 12:45 A.M. spotted a large black car paused at the intersection between the asphalt road to the ferry and the dirt road leading to the fatal bridge. The large black car's license plate, Deputy Sheriff Look remembered, began with "L7." The Kennedy car, a black Oldsmobile, had license number L78207. The Deputy Sheriff immediately identified it as the one he had spotted at 12:45, after it was hauled out of the pond. Look's sighting of it conflicts with Kennedy's version of the time of the accident and also brings into question the real purpose of his nocturnal foray. Allegedly, it was to take Mary Jo to the ferry—but the last ferry had already departed at midnight, forty-five minutes before Look spotted what he insists was the Kennedy car. Also, if Kennedy's car paused deliberately at the intersection of the asphalt road to the ferry and the dirt road to the bridge, his claim that he took a hurried, mistaken turn onto the dirt road is suspect at best . . .

But the contradictions, ambiguities and enigmas are endless, and have already been the subject of scores of articles and at least five complete books, all of which raise more questions than they answer. Setting aside for the moment all questions about the veracity of Kennedy's account (and it is dubious at best on many points), how did he come up with his story? The full version was not contained in the terse 240-word statement Teddy gave Chief Arena the morning after the accident. It was unveiled in his highly emotional television address "to the people of Massachusetts" delivered a week later, after he had been coached, counseled and scripted by key members of the old Camelot Brain Trust including former Defense Secretary Robert McNamara, New Frontier ghostwriters Ted Sorensen and Richard Goodwin, and long-time Kennedy loyalist Kenneth O'Donnell. This carefully tooled speech included the melodramatic accounts of repeated dives to rescue Mary Jo, a great deal of inspirational rhetoric and little if any supporting evidence.

The inquest, which did not take place until half a year later, was closed to the press and the public—at Teddy's request. Its transcript was suppressed for another three months. The judge, James Boyle, had previously said that he did not feel that Kennedy should be "further" punished. Despite this prejudicial remark he did not disqualify himself from presiding over the inquest. But even Judge Boyle's findings included a "presumption of fact" that at least a part of Teddy's account of the accident was untrue—that he had *intentionally* turned off the asphalt road and the route to the ferry (his alleged destination) onto the dirt road leading to Dyke Bridge where the accident occurred:

> I believe it probable [concluded Judge Boyle] that Kennedy knew of the hazard that lay ahead of him on Dyke Road but that, for some reason not apparent from the testimony, he failed to exercise due care as he approached the bridge.
>
> I therefore find there is probable cause to believe that Edward M. Kennedy operated his motor vehicle negligently . . . and that such operation appears to have contributed to the death of Mary Jo Kopechne.

He then dropped the case, although, under the law, such a finding could have been expected to lead to arrest and trial. At least one Kennedy intimate, Teddy's brother-in-law and current campaign manager, Steve Smith, has been quoted as saying that Kennedy's main problem at the time was riding out "the still possible charge of manslaughter."

Teddy, with a little help from his friends, rode it out.

There are all sorts of sinister counterexplanations of the events at Chappaquiddick, some of them at least as plausible as Teddy's on a theoretical basis. Others have already developed them, and we can be sure that a rash of new paperbacks on the subject will not be long in reaching the stands as the 1980 race proceeds. For the purposes of considering Teddy's fitness for a high position of public trust, however, his own account of his conduct—and the discrepancies and gaps it contains—are serious enough. Writing in 1976, liberal author Sherrill called it "a case study of how a famous politician—by delays, by obfuscation, by propaganda, by all sorts of tricks and wiles—can kill somebody under mysterious circumstances and still regularly receive more than 40 percent of the support in presidential preference polls."

The only thing that has changed since 1976 is the polls—and they've been going *up* for Teddy. As for the episode itself, when Kennedy officially began his campaign for the 1980 nomination 80 percent of the public claimed to remember Chappaquiddick, but no more than 20 percent of the electorate said it would cause them to vote against him—and many of these were Republican or conservative voters who would probably not vote for Kennedy in any event. Time, as H.L. Mencken once observed, is a great legalizer, even in the field of morals.

Still, Chappaquiddick is there—an iceberg issue measurable at the surface, but of unknown dimensions beneath the waterline. And, as I will point out in discussing Teddy's *Wild Card* factor, it has led to other rumors, allegations and inquiries into his character and personal fitness that could seriously damage him as a candidate. For the moment, however, let F. Scott Fitzgerald, the greatest American chronicler of lost souls and empty beautiful people, have the last word. About the same time that I began my research on Kennedy and his entourage, I happened to be rereading *The Great Gatsby,* where I came across a short descriptive passage that seemed to sum up the thoughtless, amoral attitude of some wealthy, powerful people toward us ordinary mortals, especially when we prove to be an inconvenience to them.[2]

There were plenty of these arrogant, gilded barbarians around in the twenties and thirties when Gatsby—and Old Joe Kennedy, the Godfather of the family—were making their bundles by stock jobbing and liquor distribution, licit or il. Pa Kennedy was one of the most ruthless, opportunistic wheeler dealers in a ruthless, opportunistic era, and he trained his brood well. Hence the apposite passage from Fitzgerald:

> They were careless people . . . they smashed up things and creatures and then retreated back into their money or their vast carelessness, or whatever it was that kept them together, and let other people clean up the mess they had made.

In his human relationships and personal ethics, as in his pragmatic political instincts, Teddy seems to be even more his father's son than either Jack or Bobby was.

So much, for now, of Chappaquiddick and all that it stands for. Before returning to it under Teddy's *Wild Card* factor, let's see how he measures up on the other six *Deadly Whims*.

KENNEDY LEADERSHIP (Whim 1)

"Leadership" is the unofficial theme of the Kennedy campaign. In one of his first speeches on the stump, Teddy used the words "leader" and "leadership" no less than seventeen times. Although he never singled out Jimmy Carter by name, his three-tiered message was clear:

[2]By an odd coincidence, I later discovered that Robert Sherrill was also so struck by the same quote's relevance to Teddy Kennedy and family that he chose it as the title page theme for his book, *The Last Kennedy* (Dial Press, 1976).

1. America needs leadership in the White House.
2. Jimmy Carter isn't providing it.
3. Teddy can.

But what sort of leadership record does *Teddy* have? Not even his fondest admirers have ever claimed that Kennedy is a dynamic leader in the self-made sense. The family fortune, family influence and family name ruled that out through no choice of his own. But behind the inherited wealth, position and popularity, were there any early signs of raw talent? One searches in vain. Youngest sons of wealthy families often have a hard time growing up, and Teddy faced the double burden of being overshadowed not only by a famous, domineering father, but also by three dynamic older brothers: Joe Jr., whom the head of the family had originally slotted for the Presidency but who was killed in World War II; Jack, his successful understudy; and Bobby. Most people who knew Joe, Jack and Bobby agree that, besides having a headstart on Teddy in years, all three were also his superior in gray matter.

Outgunned as an achiever, Teddy did what many another rich kid in his situation did—he goofed off. The young playboy was caught cheating and left Harvard under a cloud in 1951 (returning later to complete his undergraduate work and afterwards earning a law degree at the University of Virginia). His only other remarkable achievement during his youthful years was an impressive string of speeding tickets. Dick Tuck, the celebrated Democratic "political prankster" who played an active role in Jack Kennedy's successful campaign for the Presidency, recalls that in 1960 Kennedy insiders dismissed Teddy as "Jack's younger brother, who . . . had the somewhat ambiguous title of campaign coordinator for the eleven western states. When something was happening in California, Teddy would be in Colorado. Jack didn't carry a single state in the region, although you really couldn't blame Teddy for that. He had nothing to do with it."

Before running for the Senate in Massachusetts in 1962, the 30-year-old Teddy's sole experience in public service had been as a $1-a-year member of the Suffolk County Massachusetts District Attorney's staff. He tried exactly one case. Still the Kennedy name worked its magic, and Teddy defeated State Attorney General Edward McCormack, a far more qualified and experienced candidate for the Senate nomination and then went on to swamp his feeble Republican opponent. Perhaps the tenor of Teddy's first serious plunge into politics was best captured in a single angry, despairing remark Edward McCormack made during a televised debate with Kennedy: "I ask, since the question of names and families has been injected, if his name was Edward Moore, with his qualifications—with your qualifications, Teddy—if it was Edward Moore, your candidacy would be a joke. But nobody's laughing because his name is not Edward Moore. It's Edward Moore Kennedy."

And so, as Dick Tuck put it in a recent *Washington Post* article, "in 1962, his brother and the generous people of Massachusetts gave him a Senate seat, and some would say that they were spoiling him." Now there is nothing unique about using family pull, money or popularity for an easy start in politics. Many great leaders in history have done so, only to prove individual talent of a high order afterwards—Julius Caesar, Winston Churchill and Franklin Roosevelt, to mention only three. But until the murder of his two brothers forced him to take up the mantle of family leadership, Teddy remained a frivolous figure. In the words of Dick Tuck, the young Senator from Massachusetts "chased around with college roommates and with cousins whose only responsibilities were to open the summer houses, and who usually forgot the keys."

The first indication of any higher ambition on Teddy's part was his upset victory over Russell Long for the post of Senate Majority Whip in 1969. Ironically, Long was then vulnerable because of inattention to detail and a drinking problem (he has since pulled himself together and is one of the most influential members of the Senate). The same two reasons were given behind the scenes when Teddy himself was turned out of the post by his colleagues in 1972 and replaced by Senator Robert Byrd of West Virginia. On the basis of the public record and the votes of his Democratic peers, Teddy was a failure as a leader in the Senate. However, whatever else was going on inside him after the triple traumas of two family assassinations and Chappaquiddick, he did muster enough inner strength to gradually salvage his reputation within the Senate chamber, as a member if not a leader. While he has not built up a solid record of achievement as a maker of laws, Teddy's committee work as Chairman of the Senate Judiciary Committee, the Labor and Human Resources Subcommittee on Health and Scientific Research and the Joint Economic Subcommittee on Energy has won him frequent praise (and a certain amount of collegial jealousy) for his hard work and efficient staff operation. He is also personally well-liked by many of his colleagues on both sides of the aisle.

In contrast to his only modestly successful record of real leadership, Teddy's publicly perceived leadership qualities as a dynamic Kennedy still stand high. They are an important source of strength for him in the polls. Especially among Democratic voters, he is *seen* as a strong leader—much more so than Carter. If he can sustain this perception through what is bound to be a bitter campaign, he will maintain his important lead over Carter in Whim 1, whether or not his actual record of leadership warrants it.

KENNEDY COMMUNICATION (Whim 2)

As I pointed out in my evaluation of Jimmy Carter, he and Teddy have exactly opposite problems with communication. Carter can think on his feet with a fair amount of speed and clarity and is a better than average debater and interviewee. Kennedy on the other hand gets high marks as a reader or memorizer of ghosted speeches (and has a superior stable of ghostwriters to provide them), but often falls apart impromptu. His extremely weak performance during a CBS television interview with Roger Mudd in November of 1979 was so bad that it was quickly dubbed "Teddy's Mudslide" in journalistic circles. It embarrassed many of his family's staunchest admirers and may have turned off or at least raised serious misgivings among millions of rank-and-file Democrats. Much to their amazement, Teddy's fans—many of them watching him in a tough, unrestricted interview for the first time— discovered that their hero even had trouble explaining why he wanted to be President. In response to Roger Mudd's obvious and predictable question, Teddy waffled, wavered and wandered:

> Well, I'm—were I to make the announcement, and to run, the reasons that I would run is [sic] because I have a great belief in this country, that is—there's more natural resources than any nation of the world; there's the greatest educated population in the world; greatest technology of any country in the world; and the greatest political system in the world. . . . And the energies and the resourcefulness of this nation, I think, should be focused on these problems in a way that brings a sense of restoration—in this country by its people to—in dealing with the problems we face. Primarily the issues on the economy, the problems of— energy. And—I would basically feel that—that it's imperative for this country to either move forward; that it can't stand still or otherwise it moves backwards.

This fractured physics lesson, which made Jerry Ford sound like Demosthenes in retrospect, had nothing to do with why Teddy should be President, and it prompted the *Washington Star*'s resident Kennedy cultist, Mary McGrory, to lament that his television interviews "show another weakness. Away from the prepared text, Kennedy is halting, rambling and uncertain, when he starts a sentence, of where it will end. He could in debate, the White House must be thinking, do the impossible; that is, make murmuring Jimmy Carter sound crisp and forceful."

Shortly afterwards, Carter—who must read the *Star*—agreed to debate with Kennedy. Thus the same communications tool that Jack Kennedy used to defeat Richard Nixon in 1960 could, twenty years later, boomerang on his younger brother. As a communicator Teddy comes out somewhere in the middle, his ability to give a good rehearsed reading on the stump or on camera countered by his weakness as an intelligent, articulate impromptu speaker. Dissecting one of Teddy's meandering responses during the Mudd interview, columnist Bill Buckley concluded: "That paragraph sounds distressingly like one of those student papers people are always printing to document the charge that 16-year-olds are illiterate." Unlike his older brothers, Teddy runs into trouble when he has to fall back on his own vocabulary and his own ideas. This makes the skill of the men around him—his writers, organizers, strategists and advisors—an even more crucial factor than it is with most candidates.

KENNEDY ORGANIZATION (Whim 3)

Whereas Jimmy Carter has only a small core of comparatively inexperienced Georgia cronies like Gerald Rafshoon, Jody Powell and Ham Jordan, Teddy Kennedy can pick and choose loyalist supporters who embrace three political generations: veterans who cut their teeth in Jack Kennedy's 1960 race and subsequent "thousand days" in the White House; members of the class of '68 who worked for Bobby and would probably have won the Democratic nomination for him if Sirhan Sirhan had been a poorer shot; and Teddy's own able cadre of Senate, committee and campaign staffers. Add to all these a wide array of prominent academics in fields like economics, political science and foreign affairs—all of them attracted by the smell of power and the Kennedy mystique, and many of them happening to hail from Teddy's alma mater, Harvard— and you come up with a pretty impressive talent lineup.

It is really amusing, the lengths to which some of these exalted intellects will go to earn a few brownie points with Kennedy. Ordinarily serious, intelligent men like historian Arthur Schlesinger, Jr., hopeful of once more winning entrée to the White House, lose all shame in their panegyrics of Teddy. Schlesinger, for one, had already begun making the rounds of the television talk shows, touting his latest Kennedy patron before he had even announced his candidacy. Schlesinger's professed esteem for Teddy is boundless, as is his willingness to look at the sunny side of even the shadiest parts of the Kennedy record. Thus according to Schlesinger, Chappaquiddick, far from being a blot in Teddy's copy book, was an inspiring experience, a time when "the iron went into Edward Kennedy's soul."

More important than the hollow apologetics and transparent puffery of Teddy's intellectual hangers-on is the calibre of his *real* lieutenants—the ones who will run his campaign. And here Kennedy seems to be able to choose well. Conflicting loyalties at the top are no problem; the man running his campaign, New York attorney and political operative Steve Smith, is also Teddy's brother-in-law, the husband of his older sister, Jean. Smith has a reputation as a tough, canny infighter good at maintaining discipline in the ranks and capable of saying "no" with confidence that his decisions will be backed by the boss. He is also a very capable businessman who has had a large hand in managing the Kennedy family fortune over the years. At 51, Smith has lived down his earlier image as a hard-drinking partygoer and was recently described by a friend as having turned into "a middle-aged sherry drinker." He has also been praised as a fund raiser who "can pick up the phone and raise a million bucks."

While there will be a sprinkling of other Camelot veterans in the Kennedy organization as it expands, most of the senior staff, aside from Smith, are younger and more liberal than brother Jack's cold war warriors. Mainly in their thirties and early forties, Teddy's inner circle includes Paul Kirk, a trusted political counselor; Carl Wagner, a liberal political organizer with strong labor ties and a nationwide network of contacts with Democratic officeholders and local political bosses; Richard G. Stearns, a Massachusetts lawyer and former McGovern backer with a reputation as a keen delegate hunter; Dick Drayne, now a Washington consultant but formerly Teddy's press secretary and still a part-time advisor and speechwriter; his legislative assistant, Carey Parker, who has serious input into most of Kennedy's policy stands; and Dr. Larry Horowitz, a bright young physician who helped Teddy shape his national health insurance plan.

Youthful, liberal, intelligent and aggressive, Kennedy's team also has a reputation for a certain amount of arrogance and ruthlessness—but this was also true of his older brothers' operators, and it seemed to enhance rather than weaken their political effectiveness. One staff weakness, given the fact that more than half of the delegates to the 1980 Democratic Convention will be women, is the male chauvinist slant reflected in Teddy's "kitchen cabinet." Kennedy doesn't seem to be comfortable delegating serious responsibility to woman aides, and few if any occupy senior slots. This, taken with his personal reputation as a love 'em and leave 'em Don Juan of the old school, could cost him some points with liberal but liberated woman voters.

On the whole, however, Teddy gets high marks for his staff, and will probably continue to pick up both able technicians and big-name drawing cards as his campaign progresses. Old

Kennedy loyalties and superior organization have already won him frontrunner status in two key states—Illinois and Pennsylvania. In both cases, it was the old, city-based machines that led the swing from Carter to Kennedy. In Chicago, Mayor Jane Byrne and Cook County Democratic Chairman George W. Dunne were early Kennedy endorsers, which means, as pundits Roland Evans and Robert Novak were quick to report, that "Carter begins the battle for Illinois's 179 delegates with Chicago in Senator Edward Kennedy's pocket. Since the President can at best hope for an even split of downstate delegates, his prospects are bleak next March 18 in the very primary labeled essential by his own agents."

Indeed, Illinois could be the *coup de grace* for Carter, if Kennedy can manage to win not only the early northeastern primaries, but the March 11 Florida Primary as well. If he does, Jimmy Carter may never recover from the lethal one-two-three punch.

Consider, too, the state of Pennsylvania. In 1976 it was Jimmy Carter's primary victory in Pennsylvania that sewed up the nomination for him. But in 1980 Philadelphia, the single largest source of Democratic strength in the Keystone State, is solidly behind Kennedy. He has the backing of many of former Mayor Frank Rizzo's hard-line lieutenants as well as the new, liberal Democratic mayor and long-time Kennedy friend, William Green. Also in the Kennedy camp is Carter's former Deputy Attorney General, ex-Pittsburgh mayor Pete Flaherty—a man credited with being one of the architects of Carter's 1976 Pennsylvania victory. The same shift to Kennedy, sometimes at a walk and sometimes at a gallop, is occurring throughout the country in many key Democratic party organizations. And where the pros go, the money soon follows.

KENNEDY WAR CHEST (Whim 4)

Besides Morris Dees, the former Carter fundraiser who defected to Kennedy in 1979, and campaign chief Steve Smith himself, Teddy has other powerful fundraising expertise— Martin Katz, an expert fundraiser who formerly worked for Senator Daniel Patrick Moynihan of New York to cite but one example. And performance told. In the first four days after its official opening, Teddy's campaign committee had already raised a quarter of a million dollars in contributions.

National organization aside, there are also many local and state-wide backers whom the Kennedy forces can call on for quick results when needed. Thus, when the word went out to South Dakota in late 1979 that Kennedy backers there needed to quickly raise $5,000 in individual contributions of $250 or less to make South Dakota one of twenty states qualifying Teddy for matching federal campaign funding, former Lt. Governor Bill Dougherty was back with the money, and an extra thousand to spare, in less than a week. So far, the Carter organization hasn't been able to match this kind of efficiency, partially because the people who are best at the work, like Dougherty, are often old Kennedy and McGovern backers who have already written off Carter.

So Teddy outscores Jimmy Carter in the war chest department, despite the latter's inherent advantage as a sitting President. Unlike Jimmy Carter, Teddy also has substantial private means to fall back on in an emergency—to the extent that he can reconcile use of the family millions with stiffer new election spending laws. One thing is certain, the money is there if he needs it and can find ways of channeling it into his campaign. By 1976 the Kennedys had already spent an estimated minimum of $14 million on various family campaigns—and there was plenty more where that came from. As that redoubtable matriarch Rose Kennedy once snapped back at a reporter who asked about this massive family political spending: "It's our money, isn't it?"

KENNEDY AGE/HEALTH (Whim 5)

The Kennedy family record for candor on health matters is rather dismal. Jack Kennedy's dependence on cortisone to combat Addison's disease was successfully concealed in 1960 when it could have been a damaging revelation in a remarkably close election. Teddy, however, seems to have little to hide. At 47 he is not only healthy but robust. Except for the back brace he wears as a result of injuries sustained in a plane crash, Teddy's only noticeable problem in recent years has been overweight, and even that seems to be under control for the time being. He has always shown plenty of aggressive stamina as a campaigner and the only significant medical treatment he is known to have received recently was the removal of a small cancerous lesion from his chest in June of 1979. Unless there was more to that operation than it appears, Teddy deserves a clean bill of health. Given equal overall condition, he would still enjoy a slight edge over Carter in this department because of the eight year difference in their ages and the deeply imbedded public perception of the Kennedys as the embodiment of political and personal "vigah."

KENNEDY MARRIAGE/FAMILY (Whim 6)

Of all the 1980 candidates, Republican and Democratic, Teddy is the one with the most complex marriage/family reading. To judge from the record he is a loving, loyal son and parent, but a rather inadequate, errant husband—and the public will doubtless be treated to more and more personal details, both favorable and unfavorable, as the campaign progresses.

All but the most inveterate Kennedy haters must feel a pang of pity for a family that has suffered so much tragedy in public life, whether or not one has a very high opinion of the

Kennedy contribution to the political process. If there is crudity in the dynastic pursuit of power, there is also courage and determination in the face of danger. How much credit Teddy deserves for the sacrifices of other members of his family is debatable on an ethical plane, but there is no doubt that many, perhaps a majority of Americans, think of themselves as indebted to the Kennedys. And Teddy is the only Kennedy left to collect on the emotional debt.

When 24-year-old David Kennedy, one of Bobby's sons, was involved in a dope scandal in the autumn of 1979, the public reaction was one of sympathy rather than disgust. Besides, considering their numbers and the traumas they have undergone, most of the Kennedy kids have held up pretty well. Caroline and John, Jr., are both almost alarmingly normal young people—pleasant, low-key and anything but obsessive. Robert Kennedy, Jr., though sometimes rabid in his political statements, is intelligent and seemingly bent on a serious political career. And Teddy's oldest son, Edward, Jr., has fought a heroic battle against the cancer that cost him a leg.

Joan Kennedy, Teddy's wife, presents a more complex factor. Her serious drinking and mental problems, and the disintegration of their marriage could gain Kennedy further sympathy—or could reflect poorly on him as a husband. The failure of the marriage and Joan's health problems, one close friend recently told society writer Judy Bachrach, is "90 percent his fault." Whatever the reason, the once beautiful Joan is now a nervous, haggard introvert. Anyone who watched her performance in Boston when Teddy, having announced his candidacy, called her up to the microphone to state her willingness to campaign for him, will never forget the anguish in her expression, and the difficulty she had controlling her facial muscles. Living alone in her Boston apartment, apart from her husband, her children and the overpowering presence of her numerous inlaws, Joan Kennedy seems to be desperately working at putting her life back together. Whether Teddy's real or suspected infidelities and Chappaquiddick were partially responsible for driving her over the edge in the first place is something we may never know. But the suspicion that it was will probably cost Teddy a few votes, and certainly injects a negative factor into his *Marriage/Family* equation.

WILD CARD (Whim 7)

The biggest negative Kennedy wild card is, of course, Chappaquiddick—not merely the incident itself, but the cloud of uncertainty it has generated about Teddy Kennedy's credibility and character. It is virtually impossible to measure the intensity of it in advance of real voting. And even then, separating Chappaquiddick from political issues may prove difficult, especially since many people, when polled, show a marked reticence on the subject or a tendency to deny that it is a factor unless asked about it indirectly. Meg Greenfield, *Newsweek* magazine's liberal columnist, put the problem in as clear a perspective as anyone could when she wrote:

> I believe Kennedy's closer friends and staff and supporters who argue that this [Chappaquiddick] is a concern only to soreheads, cranks and a few right-wing bananas do him a terrible disservice. What happened that night and the senator's attitude toward it and conduct thereafter presents a legitimate subject of interest and anxiety and casts a huge moral shadow over his candidacy. It emerges as a failure of personal and public responsibility so large and deep as to overwhelm much of the undeniable goodness and strength of the man.

Another long-time Kennedy admirer who shares Ms. Greenfield's misgivings is New York author Jimmy Breslin. After watching the Roger Mudd interview he concluded:

If Kennedy persists, if he wants to seem distant and uncaring about his own failure there, he could start people who generally have decided that Chappaquiddick is not reason enough to vote against him into looking at each other and saying, "If this guy doesn't care about what happened to the girl, then why is he going to care about me and my kids?"

As long as the public continues to disbelieve Kennedy's version of the facts on Chappaquiddick, he tends to lose the benefit of the doubt when other allegations—especially concerning his private life—are made. Whether these deserve to be an issue or not, they will be. And one that could hurt Teddy most with a group of voters the Kennedys used to be able to take for granted—young-to-middle-aged, blue collar parents, many of them Catholic, who still hold strong views on what is and is not moral.

The sort of fresh scandal that could be in store for Kennedy is typified by a little-noticed item that appeared in England last autumn in *Private Eye.* Despite the scabrous ring to its name, *Private Eye* is not a low-class scandal sheet. It is a provocative, investigative political weekly that has repeatedly broken stories Fleet Street's more staid publications were afraid to handle, and its contributors include many of the top reporters for stolid journals like the *Daily Telegraph,* the *Times* and the *Guardian* who pass on items that their parent papers may be afraid to run. One should also bear in mind that the British laws for libel are much stricter than their American equivalents, and *Private Eye* therefore has to be much more cautious about what it publishes than American periodicals. On the other hand, the publishers of *Private Eye* don't need to worry about staying on speaking terms with Kennedy or any other American politician who might end up President, which places them under less self-interested restraint. Whatever the reason, the story, which ran in the September 28, 1979 issue of *Private*

Eye, gave a very detailed account of an alleged incident during a 1976 Kennedy visit to Athens involving the Grand Bretagne Hotel, drugs, a young female exchange student from a prominent American banking family and the Greek police. While widely discussed in Europe at the time (I happened to be in Vienna when it surfaced) it has never, to my knowledge, been picked up or investigated by any American newspaper or the electronic media.

I cite the article, not because I am sure of its accuracy, but as an example of the kind of lurid rumors that are rampant about Kennedy on both sides of the Atlantic and have already found their way into print overseas in a major publication subject to stringent British libel laws.

Like it or not, we can probably expect a growing barrage of this sort of thing here in the United States if the race for the nomination and the White House is as long and bitter as now seems likely. And because Teddy's personal credibility has already been called into question by Chappaquiddick, even the most unsavory charges will find some believers, whether they are fully proven or not.

This is a subject I have found it distasteful to write about, but I am convinced that it is going to have a significant though as yet unmeasurable impact on the campaign. Therefore I could not ignore it in assessing Teddy Kennedy's *chances,* whether or not it has any bearing on his *fitness.*

Fate has dealt Kennedy another cruel wild card, and one that is even more painful to discuss—the assassination factor. If, as many psychologists now suggest, recent political assassins and would-be assassins in America have been psychotic "loners" like Oswald, Sirhan, Ray and Bremer—insignificant little men trying to win recognition for themselves by destroying a famous, magnetic figure—is there then such a thing as an assassination domino effect? When one misfit gained a grim sort of immortality by killing Jack Kennedy, did that trigger the impulse in a number of other "suggestible" psychotics, one of whom (Sirhan Sirhan) eventually murdered Bobby Kennedy? And when Sirhan succeeded, did his act trigger the impulse in even more potential assassins to be the one to get the last of the Kennedy brothers?

It is a horrible thing even to think about. But it, too, affects the odds, as a potential hazard to Teddy's successful candidacy. Kennedy himself has thought about the problem, and when a friend warned him that, in all probability, "somebody's out there waiting for you," Teddy reportedly shrugged and responded, "They could be waiting for me even if I weren't running for President."

He is probably right, though the emotional hype of a presidential race probably inflames the negative emotions of a potential assassin just as it excites supporters in a positive way. Ironically, what may lower the risk of yet another Kennedy tragedy is the fact that Teddy lacks some of his two brothers' dynamism and personal magnetism. His inability to kindle quite the same burning enthusiasm among his supporters that Jack and Bobby did may also mean that he is a less emotionally riveting target for deranged killers.

Taken in all, then, Kennedy emerges with a distinct but far from overwhelming edge over Jimmy Carter—a substantial initial advantage on *Leadership;* an almost equal set of *Communication* strengths and weaknesses; superior *Organization* and *War Chest;* a minuscule lead on *Age/Health;* a mixed but essentially positive *Marriage/Family* reading; and, unlike Carter, strongly negative *Wild Card* factors.

Before moving on to Jerry Brown, a final word or two on Kennedy as a figure in the historical drama. All of his life, Teddy has been forced by circumstances to follow in the footsteps of his father and brothers. Even in becoming a candidate for President, he is still a prisoner of the cycle without which, I am convinced, he would probably be a fatter, happier, much less famous member of the United States Senate—at the very most. While Teddy made the conscious decision to run in 1980, it can be argued that it was really only his ultimate surrender to outside pressures that have been pushing him into the arena from the moment Bobby was assassinated. As the last of the brothers, he is a one-man industry, with literally thousands of political, academic, and ideological dependents—many of them hacks but a considerable number of them figures of real stature. Most of them have spent the years since 1968 telling Teddy how indispensable he is to the country (by which they really mean themselves), and how only he can once more place government in the hands of the brightest and the best (again meaning themselves).

Teddy has already paid an enormous emotional price for the status rewards of being a Kennedy. But the race he has now embarked upon is going to be an even greater emotional drain. And in his inability to explain *why* he has taken on this great new burden—witness his inarticulate rambling when asked in the Mudd interview—one can detect an inner ambivalence about the race, and perhaps a lurking, deep-seated doubt about his worthiness for the office. Where Jimmy Carter over-estimates his qualifications for the Presidency and the degree to which his character morally entitles him to the office, I believe that Teddy Kennedy, underneath the family bravado and the inbred compulsion to compete, is an uneasy runner—a lonely, uncertain man whose life's course has always been controlled by others. Win or lose, he will probably spend the rest of his life as a prisoner in his Camelot shell.

3. JERRY BROWN: California Crude

*From the sublime to the ridiculous
is but a step.*

—N. Bonaparte

"IN THE YEAR 2000," California Governor Jerry Brown is fond of reminding his audiences, "I will be younger than Ronald Reagan is today." The question posed by some of the maverick California governor's critics is whether he will have grown up by then. Can this curious mix of novel but intelligent ideas and meandering claptrap manage to work out his inner contradictions and become a serious national leader with a program, or will he, like so many abortive political *Wunderkinds,* simply sink over the western horizon like a deflating hot-air balloon?

Either way, it will take time—more time than is left before the 1980 Democratic Convention, at which the best Jerry Brown can now hope to do is play the role of a major irritant to both Carter and Kennedy. It was not always so. Until Teddy's entry into the race in November of 1979, Brown was taken very seriously indeed as a presidential contender. Because of the angry "Anything But Carter" mood sweeping Democratic ranks, the national media fastened on the only Democratic celebrity clearly, though unofficially, in the running against the beleaguered incumbent.

Those were salad days for Jerry Brown, days that may never come again. Even reporters who considered the very idea of Brown in the White House frightening found him irresistible copy. Richard Reeves caught the media mood perfectly in March of '79 when he wrote:

> Most political reporters think that Jerry Brown is dangerously cynical and a little crazy. Among themselves, the people who have covered Brown's perpetual campaigning talk with real fear about what he might do or not do as president of the United States.
>
> That doesn't mean that the press will destroy Brown— or even try to. The man, for all I can tell, seems to be damn near indestructible anyway. Who else could consistently project himself as the nation's leading antipolitician when he has spent his entire adult life running for political office? The presidential campaign Brown is on now is his sixth run since 1968. He runs, I'm convinced, to escape the boredom symptomatic of his cynicism.

Cynicism may be too harsh a word, or not the right one. Mischievousness might come a little closer. Jerry Brown seems to take a perverse delight in titillating the voters and annoying his fellow politicians, and why shouldn't he? Everyone's entitled to a little fun now and then, and Brown, who takes little or no interest in food, drink, family, sex, music, friendship or even stamp collecting, does enjoy lecturing other people and raising their hackles. He is not a warm, affectionate sort of fellow, but he does love an audience. And once Jerry Brown gets his hands on one, there is no stopping him. When he runs out of real things to talk about, he just goes on, casting such perplexing pearls to the multitude as:

> I see the world in very fluid, contradictory, emerging, interconnected terms, and with that kind of circuitry I just don't feel the need to say what is going to happen or will not happen. . . . It's the circuitry of semiconductors and computers and electronic interconnections, that's what's happening today.

Hmm. Is there more here than meets the ear, or less? At face value it sounds like a rehash of 1910 Italian futurism as told to the editors of *Popular Mechanics.* But that sort of thing sometimes sells well, especially in California—mass-marketed pseudophilosophy expressed in technical crudities equally simple (or inscrutable) to the layman and the lama.

And then, just as one is about to consign Jerry Brown to the flake file, he invariably says something that does make sense. He expresses concern about the decline in positive social institutions such as schools, neighborhoods and the family. He decries one of California's biggest exports, the "do your own thing" lifestyle as: "antithetical to the service of God. Pop psychology lets people expect they can be high twenty-four hours a day. The idea of duty is that there are certain rules you are supposed to follow and you just follow them. That is falling apart in some cases." And in the next breath, Brown opposes reimposition of the draft—about the only universal "duty" available to society other than paying taxes.

"We serve the people by empowering them to regain greater control over their government," he declared in his November 8th declaration of candidacy. But Jerry Brown is all for continuing the current massive regulatory powers of the federal government and wants to add more government planning and controls, especially affecting the economy.

His motto, which could have come directly from the studio

set of the Star Ship *Enterprise,* is: "Protect the earth, serve the people and explore the universe." But, while pouring fresh billions into space exploration, he also wants to call a Constitutional Convention to pass a balanced budget amendment that would make most or all of his proposed new programs unaffordable. When pressed on this point, Jerry Brown concedes that his support for the convention idea is only "a metaphor."

He is the Captain of the Metaphor, and a right good captain, too—drifting on gossamer sails from one airy, half-formed notion to another, but never running aground. What, never? Well, hardly ever. "We have an economy that creates things that fall apart," Jerry Brown complains, inadvertently giving a good description of what he is doing in the realm of ideas.

But let us forsake the worthy Captain Brown's mystical metaphors and mind-boggling metaphysics for the nonce and take a look at the man and his real strengths and weaknesses as a candidate.

Jerry Brown suffers from congenital politics. Born on April 7, 1938, he is the son of Edmund "Pat" Brown of California, an affable, old-fashioned liberal politician who is probably best remembered for defeating Richard Nixon in the race for the governor's mansion in 1962. Young Jerry seems to have fought his genes for a few years, opting for a religious life. In 1956 he entered the Jesuit Order's Sacred Heart Novitiate. Discipline was hard. Jerry must have found the restriction on novices talking to each other particularly vexing. He has certainly made up for that early embargo on the spoken word since. In 1960 he left the seminary for Berkeley, and he hasn't stopped talking since.

But though Jerry Brown gave up the idea of becoming a priest, he preserves his Jesuitical love of debate and hairsplitting to this day, along with an ascetic taste for bare surroundings and contemplation that has since been strengthened by his dabbling in Zen Buddhism. Hardly your average ward heeler.

By 1961 he had earned a Bachelor of Arts degree at Berkeley and in 1964 he received his law degree from Yale. After clerking for a California State Supreme Court justice and joining a Los Angeles law firm, Jerry yielded to the call of the wild, gradually immersing himself in the civil rights and antiwar movements. In 1968 he campaigned for Eugene McCarthy and, a year later, won his own first elective office as a member of the Board of Trustees of the Los Angeles community colleges. He never looked back, winning the post of California Secretary of State in 1970 and narrowly defeating Republican Houston Flournoy for the governorship in 1974, when GOP fortunes were at low ebb in California thanks to Watergate.

Brown's first years as governor were productive, whether or not one happened to agree with his flirtation with Cesar Chavez and other controversial policies, and he got along fairly well with the Democratic State Legislature.

Then in March of 1976 he declared himself a favorite-son candidate for the Presidency and created a stir by beating Jimmy Carter in every primary he seriously contested—Maryland, California, Nevada, Rhode Island and New Jersey. It didn't stop Carter, who already had the nomination sewed up, but it did embarrass him. And it marked the birth of Jerry Brown, national gadfly.

A more pettily consistent man than Jerry Brown might have come a cropper in 1978, the year he was up for reelection as governor. In June, Proposition 13, the controversial antitax measure which he had opposed, was approved by an overwhelming majority of California voters. Jerry simply changed sides and rode the crest of the taxpayers' revolt to a landslide reelection victory in November. Thanks to the state budget surpluses piled up by his predecessor, Ronald Reagan, Brown was able to implement Proposition 13 without many painful cuts in services and simultaneously won a reputation as the taxpayers' friend across the nation. But his own state party was beginning to resent him and to look askance at some of his more controversial appointments. In the spring 1979 session of the State Legislature, three of his vetoes were overridden in as many weeks, and the State Senate turned down his appointment of Hanoi-junketing actress Jane Fonda, to the California Arts Council.

Not that it mattered much. Jerry Brown was already busy running for President again. And as long as he was the only visible Carter opponent, things kept looking up. In a two-way race, his early strategy made sense, banking on heavy Catholic and youth support in the East and Midwest and a strong showing in the his native Southwest. In many ways, Brown's strategy was a cynical, heavy-handed updating of Carter's own in 1976—the "California Crude" version, one bemused observer of West Coast politics dubbed it. Like Jimmy Carter in '76, Brown decided to run as the clean, innovative outsider—the anti-Washington candidate—and to simultaneously woo disenchanted Democrats to Carter's left and right. The right wing would be serenaded with his budget-cutting routine, the left with his environmental and antinuclear refrains. And the media would be *talked* into submission for, as political columnist David Broder observed, "Jerry Brown is never at a loss for words. They pour from him like a mountain spring, shimmering and sparkling. Partly for his own amusement and partly for political effect, Brown juggles words and concepts that are on the frontiers of public discourse and national consciousness, probing a future of holistic medicine, renewable resources, solar power."

At the time, it was the only show running, and it played well. Then came Teddy, first with his announcement that wife and family had given him permission to run; next with the setting up of an authorized national campaign headquarters; and finally, just one day before Brown's own, with his official announcement in Boston on November 7th.

Jerry's kickoff, staged at the stately but slightly threadbare National Press Club in Washington the next day, was sheer anticlimax. He trotted out his familiar California rhetoric and imported, cheering supporters for the occasion, but the press had seen and heard it all before. His talk of America as a "vibrant, yeasty society" was old hat—especially to the huddled regulars at the Press Club bar whose drinking habits have been a daily tribute to the Yeasty Society since before Jerry Brown was born.

Worse yet, Teddy Kennedy had picked up Jerry's strategy and run with it. As far as most of the early *and* big state primaries are concerned (with the exception of California), it *still* is a two-man race—only now it's between Carter and Kennedy. All Jerry can do, unless one of the big boys steps into something very dirty very early, is nibble away at little bits of the two leading contenders' support—a few Catholics, environmentalists and antinukes from Kennedy, a few Jeffersonian Democrats who like small-budget rhetoric from Carter. Mere table scraps.

Still Jerry Brown is a candidate, and he is governor of our richest, most populous—and, some might add, most besotted—state. Whether he is a man of yesterday, today or tomorrow, he bears watching for that reason alone. Herewith his *Seven Deadly Whims* rating.

BROWN LEADERSHIP (Whim 1)

"The times call out for discipline and for vision. Because I see neither, I offer myself as a candidate for the presidency. An insurgent movement within the Democratic party to challenge the dying myths that paralyze our nation. It is time to wake up America. . . ." Thus Jerry Brown in his kickoff speech. Like Kennedy, he called for and then offered leadership. But what sort of leadership does he have to offer, both real and perceived?

Highlights of Brown's career as governor have already been offered. It seems to have gone down well in California, and there is certainly plenty of antitax sentiment around the country today. But unless Jerry Brown scores some surprise upsets (he claims that he will bump Carter out of second place in some of the earlier primaries and then come to grips with Kennedy), he isn't likely to capture the kind of coverage and momentum that will get his name across and make him look like a forceful, winning leader of national stature. Many people find Brown *interesting,* but as a potential President he is even viewed askance by most California voters. A Field Poll taken in the third quarter of 1979 among potential Democratic primary voters showed Teddy swamping Jerry by 59 percent to 17 percent, with Carter only a single point behind Brown, at 16 percent. In a one-to-one match with Kennedy, Jerry Brown rated 23 percent to Teddy's 69 percent, which shows that Kennedy was an acceptable second choice to more Carter voters than Brown was. Even facing Carter alone, Jerry Brown could only muster a plurality of 49 percent on his home turf.

If two terms as governor have not been enough to convince a majority of California Democrats that Jerry Brown is a plausible national leader, it is unlikely that a few months of campaigning around the country will create much of a nationwide boom. So poor marks to Brown on leadership.

BROWN COMMUNICATION (Whim 2)

I have already covered Jerry Brown's rhetorical style in my initial pages on him. It should be added, however, that he is a very keen debater when he doesn't let his tongue—and his sense of mischief—run away with him. Technically, he is superior to either Carter or Kennedy as a logician. But in political as opposed to formal debates, logicians, like nice guys, seldom finish first. Reasonably sound as a coached speaker for films and television, Brown comes across with a middling to good record as a communicator. His real problem is finding a nationwide audience, a cohesive theme, and the kind of funding and organization it takes to get the word out.

BROWN ORGANIZATION (Whim 3)

As governors go, Jerry Brown managed to assemble a fairly effective political staff—for running a California campaign on local issues. Now he's trying to parlay the same team into the national league. It probably won't work. The transfusion of anti-Carter operatives with national standing, and the support of disgruntled state and local party leaders around the country that might have come his way before Teddy announced, are all rallying to Camelot. All Brown has left is the vague hope of attracting a Children's Crusade *a la* Eugene McCarthy of idealist student volunteers, fleshed out with a few California pros and national party types who hate both Teddy and Jimmy. Not enough. Thomas Quinn, his campaign chairman, managed Brown's near-losing 1974 campaign in California and has since made quite a few enemies in the state as chairman of the California air resources board, He has little if any national standing in the Democratic Party. The same applies to cochairmen Richard Silberman and Richard Maullin. Out-of-state scheduling foul-ups and diplomatic bloopers have already characterized the Brown campaign, reflecting on the shoddy state of his organization. Jerry's choice of counselors can also border on the grotesque. One of his senior advisors on foreign policy was, until recently, Mr. David Karr, a sixty-year-old refugee from Brooklyn who, after a journalistic debut with the *Daily Worker,* branched out into more legitimate work as a producer, public relations man and entrepreneur specializing, curiously enough, in east-west trade deals. Shortly after spending the Fourth of July in Moscow to celebrate the opening of a new hotel he had invested in there, Mr. Karr hied his way to France, only to be found dead in his Parisian flat a few days later. So, in addition to all of his other staff woes, Jerry Brown is minus one expert on détente and disarmament—perhaps the one who talked him into his position in favor of scrubbing the MX missile system and otherwise weakening the national defense because, in Jerry's words, "I see no reason why Russia and the United States can't agree."

BROWN WAR CHEST (Whim 4)

Jerry Brown's finance chairman is Anthony Dougherty, his former legislative secretary—another gubernatorial insider with little if any clout among national Democratic fundraisers. When he declared in November of '79, Brown's committee had approximately $90,000 in the bank—hardly a drop in the bucket for a real national campaign effort. And most California contributors had either chosen between Kennedy and Carter or decided to sit out the early rounds of the match. But there were a few encouraging signs for those looking for good omens. A week earlier, the *Wall Street Journal* was able to report that Jerry Brown, the champion of "holistic healing," had attracted his biggest single bloc of contributors yet— eighty-one Chiropractors For Brown.

BROWN AGE/HEALTH (Whim 5)

Brown is lean, mean and 41. He doesn't smoke or drink and is unlikely to get fat on his meagre regimen of tacos, carry-out chow mein and "macrobiotically cooked vegetables." While his hair is slightly thinner and grayer than Ronald Reagan's, he is probably one of the physically fittest candidates in the race, both in fact and in public perception. But what a way to live!

BROWN MARRIAGE/FAMILY (Whim 6)

Although he once took a vacation in Africa with Linda Ronstadt, Jerry Brown is unmarried and shows every sign of remaining so. After all, he has the sound of his own voice to keep him warm. He is also said to be on rather distant terms with his father, who helped him get started in politics. A cold fish, Jerry, and not likely to gain any good will points on Whim 6.

BROWN WILD CARD (Whim 7)

With Jerry Brown it is probably always wise to expect the unexpected. But despite his somewhat bizarre lifestyle, there have been no seriously damaging personal scandals since he took office. Bachelors have not, historically, stood a good chance of making it to the White House. James Buchanan was the only one ever elected and he only lasted one term. But the times may be a-changin'. At any rate, Brown's private life has not yet become the kind of open game for press speculation and popular gossip that Teddy Kennedy's has—perhaps because there's so much less of it.

Earlier in his governorship, Brown's administration was rocked by serious allegations of links to organized crime, the so-called "Mexican Mafia." But none of the dirt was ever traced directly to Brown's door and the storms passed. Nevertheless one has the unscientific hunch that if Jerry Brown *does* stay in the race long enough, this time he is bound to say or do something, somewhere along the campaign trail that will antagonize or turn off a lot of non-laid-back, nonholistic, non-Californian Democrats. The risk is always there with a man like Brown who is, himself, a walking wild card.

End of Jerry Brown's *Seven Deadly Whims.* His numerically scored chart, along with the others, will be found in *Part V: Gentlemen, Place Your Bets!*

In closing the book on the last of the Democratic *Candidates 1980,* I must confess to harboring a sneaking sort of admiration for Jerry Brown. The more I examine his record the more convinced I become that he has a good head on his shoulders —but not one that was ever meant to deal rationally and understandingly with large numbers of human beings. When he pulls the public's leg—as he often has—I am amused. When he starts getting serious, I begin to worry.

At such moments I comfort myself with the thought that California is not America, and that all of the odds seem to gravitate against a Brown Presidency, at least in 1980.

But alas, as the indefatigable Jerry himself has said, in the year 2000 he will still be younger than Ronald Reagan is today. If my guess is right, he will still be running for President, too.

The mere thought of that is enough to make one envy Ronald Reagan.

PART III

The Republicans

The trouble with the Republican Party is that it has not had a new idea for thirty years.
—Woodrow Wilson
(writing 65 years ago)

There is always a certain meanness in the argument of conservatism, joined with a certain superiority in its fact.
—Ralph Waldo Emerson

For most of the fifty-one years since Herbert Hoover became the scapegoat for the Great Depression and Franklin Roosevelt created the Democrats' New Deal coalition, the Republican Party has been plunged into what Shakespeare called "downy sleep, death's counterfeit." Neither quite dead nor quite alive, the GOP has led a fitful half-life. It has never really recovered from the bite of the political tsetse fly in 1929, and its condition ever since fits the classic diagnosis of African sleeping sickness: "A serious disease, marked by fever, protracted lethargy, tremors and loss of weight [for weight read registration]."

The Republican Party doesn't die, rise up or go away—it just lies there, despite the direst prophecies of the political pundits and the false optimism of many of its hardcore supporters. In 1972 it even staged a brief rally, with Nixon capitalizing on public distaste for McGovernism to begin to forge a moderate-conservative alliance that transcended party lines. It just might have worked, but Watergate put an end to that dream along with so many others. So today the situation remains much what it has been ever since FDR; despite our much-vaunted belief in the two-party system, we really have had fifty-one years of a one-and-a-half party system, *with individual elective offices changing hands between Democrats and Republicans but the Democrats enjoying a permanent popular plurality and—with the exception of two short years under Eisenhower—a monopoly on congressional power.*

What is most interesting about the GOP in its current reduced state is not its obvious popular weakness, but the fact that, since Roosevelt's death, it has somehow managed to win four out of the past eight presidential elections and, periodically, has captured an impressive number of governorships in important and overwhelmingly Democratic states.

Part of the reason for this is the inevitable unpopularity of some Democratic incumbents, which leads to automatic turnover. As the only organized alternative to the Democrats, the Republicans are the sole beneficiaries of this. But there is another—and in my opinion more significant—reason. Because of its social composition as the party of the middle and upper-middle classes, the GOP draws on a disproportionately large chunk of America's leadership material—educated, affluent professionals and backbone bourgeoisie (local doctors, lawyers, Chamber of Commerce, Jaycee and assorted community, charity and civic types).

A third big factor—and closely related to the second— is the basic nature of the average Republican voter. If the Democratic Party is a bigger, more vigorous collective political organism than the GOP, the individual Republican voter, as befits a party that claims to stand for individual initiative, tends to be more engaged, somewhat better educated and better off, and much more likely to contribute and vote, even in low-key, nonglamour contests.

Republicans on election day, like American Indians during droughts, tend to pray for rain. Where the weather is concerned, bad news is good news for the GOP, with its unusually high turnout of registered party members and sympathizers. The explanation for this has not been missed by the more sophisticated pollsters. Thus when the Gallup organization investigated voter registration and turnout in the fall of 1979, it found that, in a representative sampling of 7,813 adults, only 69 percent were registered to vote. The lowest percentage among the registered consisted of Blacks, southerners, the 18- to 24-year-old age bracket, those with incomes under $7,000 and independents. With the exception of the independents, all of these low turnout groups are heavily Democratic in loyalty or leaning.

On the other end of the spectrum, the highest rate of registration was among citizens with a college education, 50 years old or more, with a minimum income of $20,000 —and strongly Republican. If individual Republicans do not "vote early and vote often" after the fashion of the living and the dead in Democratic Cook County, Illinois, and certain parts of Texas, they do vote punctually and consistently, thus showing a strength far beyond their numbers, especially in an age of general voter apathy.

Finally, although an overwhelming majority of Americans identify themselves as either Democrats or independents, they also consider themselves either moderate or conservative when polled on their ideological rather than party sympathies. While these terms are too vague to take literally in every case, the strong moderate-to-conservative slant of the electorate does help to explain the increasing amount of ticket splitting that has occurred in recent years, and which usually operates in favor of—you guessed it—moderate-to-conservative candidates, especially at the presidential level. More often than not, the candidates fitting this description tend to be Republicans.

Consider the last four presidential races. In 1964, the one case in which the GOP allowed its emotions to run wild and nominated a candidate much of the electorate —rightly or wrongly—perceived as an "extremist," Democrat Lyndon Johnson defeated Republican Barry Goldwater by a landslide. He who holds the middle ground holds power. Not that the winners learned much from the lesson; in 1972 the Democrats in their turn nominated George McGovern, also perceived by the electorate as an extremist, and Nixon swamped him.

Considering its smaller voter base, the GOP has been much more successful than the Democratic Party in capturing the middle ground in post-Rooseveltian presidential races. But the very term "middle ground" can be misleading if it is taken to mean the dead ideological *center rather than the largest political population cluster on the chart. The so-called middle ground in contemporary America is not really middling in the ideological sense. The political center of gravity has actually been slightly to the right of center when it comes to presidential choices in the post-Roosevelt years, whereas the ideological pull within the numerically stronger Democratic Party has been slightly (and, in the case of McGovern, more than slightly) to the left.*

Once one recognizes this, the seemingly conflicting figures of party identification and presidential voting patterns begin to make sense. Thus, using party identifi-

cation figures compiled by the University of Michigan's Survey Research Center, we find that:

> • *In 1968, when 55 percent of Americans identified themselves as Democrats or Democrat-leaning—and only 33 percent identified themselves as Republican or Republican-leaning—Democratic presidential nominee Hubert Humphrey received only 42.7 percent of the popular vote.*
>
> • *In 1972, when only 34 percent of the population identified itself as Republican or Republican-leaning—and 51 percent were Democrats or Democrat-leaning— George McGovern only carried 37.5 percent of the popular vote.*
>
> • *In 1976, when the GOP identity/sympathy figure was only 40 percent and the Democrats' stood at 52 percent, Ford almost upset Carter and received 49 percent of the popular vote.*

As election year 1980 began, the figures for party sympathy and leanings remained about the same as in 1976, but other things had changed. Jimmy Carter, who was generally perceived as a moderate with potential for taking a fresh, efficient approach to national problems in 1976, had lost much of his popular support and was in a life and death struggle for his own party's nomination. Teddy Kennedy, who led Carter in the earliest polls, was doing his best to shift from the left wing of the Democratic Party to the center. But Teddy remained—and probably will continue to remain in the eyes of a large part of the electorate—a politician of the left on the basis of his past record and most of his present stands.

If Teddy were anyone but a Kennedy—and if Carter's popularity were not subject to possible boosts between

*now and November through dynamic executive action—
all of the odds would favor a Republican victory in 1980
—if, and this is a very big "if" indeed, the GOP choice
is an attractive candidate the electorate perceives as qualified and* moderately *conservative.*

*In 1980 there are two flies in the GOP ointment, one
put there by the Democrats and the other self-inflicted.
Teddy* is *a Kennedy and, at least in the preliminary polls,
has been able to attract massive support, including that
of many Democrats and independents who identify
themselves as being "conservative." At least in the early
phases of the race, he may be able to camouflage his
liberal liability with the asset of inherited Kennedy charisma. The second hitch is Ronald Reagan, or, more particularly, the way the non-Republican public perceives
him. Like Teddy on the Democratic side, Reagan, under
the tutelage of his wily campaign strategist, John Sears,
is trying to jockey his way from the extreme wing of his
party to the broad highway of moderation. But Reagan's
entire political career has been based on his forthright
stand as an unapologetic hardliner. Justly or unjustly,
much of the press and his political opposition see him as
a Neanderthal—an image further aggravated by his advanced age. If Reagan doesn't overcome this arbitrary
labelling, he could still win the GOP nomination, but he
will face dim chances at best of winning in a general
election.*

*Yet, even if we grant Sears his ability to reposition
Reagan closer to the popular mass and therefore
strengthen his chances in November, the aging Californian still faces a critical dilemma. His strongest support
within the GOP comes from hardcore, conservative party
regulars at the grassroots level. They love Reagan for his
unblinking conservatism. If he tries to shift gears too
suddenly or too obviously with an eye to the general*

electorate—or if he attempts another transparent, Sears-inspired gimmick like his disastrous 1976 tapping of liberal Pennsylvania Senator Richard Schweiker as his Vice President designate—the troops he needs to win the nomination could easily desert him in anger for a younger, less controversial candidate with sound moderately conservative credentials—someone like George Bush. So while Reagan starts out far ahead of all his major challengers for the nomination, he is running on a tightrope.

One important asset the Republicans do have in 1980 is a vital and technically proficient national party organization. Under Chairman Bill Brock, the Republican National Committee has modernized and become much more than the makeshift retirement home for needy party hacks that most national political headquarters are most of the time. Brock, an intellectual and something of a political technocrat, successfully focused on improved fundraising and then channelled the GOP's considerable financial assets and organizational skills into party-building from the bottom up. Thus, despite its antiquated image with the public, the GOP as a national political machine *is smoother-running, more efficient and more modern than the Democratic Party. When you're number two you learn to try harder.*

Finally, I have a personal theory about when and why voters turn to the Republican Party in presidential elections. Most of them don't much like *the GOP, so it isn't out of affection. They don't much* trust *the GOP as a "friend of the people," so it isn't out of great expectations. But there are times when they look around at the state of the nation and see that it is in a bad way—and that Democrats are in charge of both the legislative and executive branches and are not doing much to cope with the problems.*

At such times—in 1952 because of an unpopular war in Korea, domestic corruption, fears of subversion and simple weariness after a generation of Democratic rule; in 1968 because of Vietnam and violence in the streets; in 1972 through fear of McGovern's extremism—voters turn to the Republican Party the way financially beleaguered members of a family might turn to a crusty old relative who happens to be a chartered accountant. The GOP is called in like a Dutch uncle to clear away some of the debris and restore a semblance of order. Then, in four to eight years, when things seem to be back to normal—or the Republicans are being blamed for a fresh mess in the White House—people vote the Democrats, their real first love, back in. As for poor uncle, he is unceremoniously packed off until the next family crisis.

I believe that, unless the GOP savages itself or chooses the wrong man, 1980—with its rising inflation, shaky international situation and seemingly bankrupt current leadership—could well be another year of the Dutch uncle.

All of these wrinkles make the Republican race for the nomination, despite the lower emotional voltage of the personalities involved, a much more complex and technically interesting contest than its Democratic counterpart. And if Ronald Reagan overcomes the stigma of age and extremism—or one of the underdogs can depose him in a comparatively graceful, bloodless coup—the Republicans, despite their feeble paper strength, could once more seize the American electoral center and take the White House.

I. RONALD REAGAN: Rusty Paladin

Politics are almost as exciting as war,
and quite as dangerous. In war you can only
be killed once, but in politics many times.
—Winston Churchill

CALL IT A coincidence, but on January 25, 1911, the U.S. cavalry galloped south to guard the neutrality of the Rio Grande as the bloody Mexican Civil War threatened to spill over into American territory. It was one of the last times that Yankee horse soldiers would ride to the sound of a certain trumpet—a symbolic last post for frontier values and a part of America's innocence. Eleven days later, while the thunder of the cavalry's hoofbeats still echoed in the popular imagination, a child was born in Middle America.

From subsequent evidence, one suspects that the babe in question entered the world with a particularly full head of auburn hair, twinkling blue eyes, wrinkled, pink cheeks and a broad grin. His parents named him Ronald Reagan, and, unlike America, he has changed remarkably little in the intervening sixty-nine years.

"Ronny Reagan really *is* what he seems to be, no more and no less," a veteran Hollywood hand who has known him as both a politician and a show-business figure told me recently. "He really *does* believe in the old verities he spouts in those speeches of his. And he proved he could be a good governor in California. If he doesn't make it to the White House it'll be because he's just too nice for national politics—a boy scout in the best and worst sense. He's got brains, energy and talent, but Ronny's too damned naive."

There may be something to both the strengths and the weaknesses expressed above, but my source, despite his professed pessimism about Reagan's future, made a point of offering his opinion only if I ran it without attribution, perhaps with an eye to future White House guest lists—even my skeptical Hollywood friend isn't that sure the old Gipper won't baffle the odds one more time.

Critics are quick to point to Reagan's age. If he succeeds in 1980, he will be the oldest man ever elected to the Presidency. His supporters counter that age without debility is not altogether objectionable in a national leader, citing such striking examples as France's Charles de Gaulle, England's Churchill and Germany's Adenauer (and conveniently overlooking the fact that all three, although they continued to lead as old men, had begun their public careers fairly young).

Age in itself does not bring wisdom or skill, but there are times when accumulated experience and a sense of history help. And Ronald Reagan, sometimes as a bystander and sometimes as a shaper, has lived through more history than any of his rivals. It is hard to realize it when one watches the tall, trim Reagan go through one of his polished performances on the platform or on the tube, but William Howard Taft was still President when he took his first breath, and Teddy Roosevelt hadn't even begun his campaign as a Bull Moose, third-party progressive. Reagan was already 6 years old when the United States launched itself as a decisive global power by entering

World War I in 1917; he was only 18 when the crash of 1929 ushered in the Great Depression; and he hadn't turned 30 when the Japanese bombed Pearl Harbor. Ronald Reagan has lived through everything from the sinking of the *Titanic* and the Russian Revolution to Korea, Vietnam and Watergate. And now he is running for the Republican presidential nomination for the third time in a dozen years. If he has kept his eyes open all of that time, he must have learned something useful.

More than any of the other major candidates, Reagan has also known what it means to be born poor and work his way up. He not only witnessed the Depression, he *felt* it—and his kick-off speech in November of 1979 reflected his deep-felt concern, his usually well-modulated voice choking up as he described the suffering of his own family in the early 1930s, declaring: "I cannot and will not stand by while inflation and joblessness destroy the dignity of our people."

One of the major ironies of the 1980 elections is that the leading liberal contender, the nominal champion of the downtrodden, is Teddy Kennedy, the son of a millionaire who entered elective politics on the shoulders of two famous brothers. Reagan, the most formidable conservative contender, was the son of hard-pressed working-class parents and had to earn an education and build successful careers in sportscasting and films from scratch. Then at the age of 55, he had to overcome the stigma of being just another empty-headed celebrity before successfully running for governor of California.

Whether one likes his style and policies or not, one must acknowledge the personal achievement involved. A weak man, a stupid man, or a man only interested in his own comfort simply could not have done it—and probably wouldn't have tried.

As reporter Lynn Rosellini concluded after recently interviewing Reagan for the *Washington Star,* "He is a good-hearted man with a million entertaining stories, delivered in an endless repertoire of accents and facial expressions. Reagan's staff adores him, and even his critics agree that he's a straight-shooter, who deals fairly and keeps his word."

The same personal response to Reagan is echoed by one of the most experienced political operatives in Washington, a former chief of congressional relations for two Presidents who was offered the direction of Reagan's 1980 nomination race but refused it: "I've never known a finer guy in politics than Ronald Reagan," he told me, "and I think he has the Republican nomination sewed up. I like him. I respect him. But I don't think he's got a ghost of a chance to be President."

With the nation in a more conservative mood than usual in 1980, this may sound a bit odd, but one comes across the same attitude among a surprising number of Republicans. Even many of Reagan's active supporters this year seem more resigned than excited about his lead position in the nomination sweepstakes. "He's earned the nomination," many of them will tell you. And then in the next breath, they'll add that they expect Teddy Kennedy to be the next President, especially if their man gets the Republican nomination. Part of the reason for their pessimism is Reagan's age and what some see as his political shallowness. Ronald Reagan, says former California State Senator Peter Behr, is "a man able to absorb facts readily. . . . But if you walked through his deepest thoughts, you wouldn't get your feet wet."

Even his idealistic motivation, what Reagan Press Secretary Jim Lake calls his deep belief that "he has a role to play for the good of the country," is counted by some as a liability. Reagan, they say, doesn't have the necessary personal hunger for power. Richard Nixon, I recall from my own days in the White House, used to call it "a fire in the belly." It is what drives most presidential candidates through all of the aggravation, humiliation, exhaustion and unpleasant foolishness of protracted campaigning. Ronald Reagan isn't that compulsive. Like Calvin Coolidge—who, in common with Reagan, always tried to get at least nine hours of sleep—his ego doesn't itch for power.

But then one could have said the same thing about George Washington if it comes to that.

Aha, but Washington—and, for that matter, Silent Cal—didn't have to face thirty-five grueling primaries and a hostile press, the skeptics will tell you. Right again, but neither of them had a smoothly oiled national organization behind him as Reagan does, or his special strength as a television candidate in an electronic age.

But before examining Ronald Reagan's specific strengths and weaknesses as a candidate vis-à-vis the *Seven Deadly Whims,* let's take a brief look at his record, personality and platform.

Born and educated in Illinois, Ronald Reagan graduated from Eureka College in 1932. Nothing could have been more natural than for the handsome, glib former varsity star to become a popular sportscaster; for the next five years he worked as one in Des Moines, Iowa. "Dutch" Reagan, as he was known to his radio audience, became something of a local celebrity and then, in 1937, he was discovered by Hollywood. Throughout the late thirties and the forties, Reagan was cast in good and not-so-good Hollywood epics, usually as a likeable, clean-cut leading man—the sort of positive but not particularly colorful character that he seems to be in real life.

Then came television, and long-running slots as the host of *General Electric Theatre* and *Death Valley Days.* The show-business years weren't all spent on camera, however. Aside from a service stint during World War II, Reagan was also active in the Screen Actors Guild, ultimately serving as its president and winning many friends—and more than a few enemies on the left—for his strong anti-Communist stand. It was his Guild experience, more than anything else, that probably turned Reagan away from his original political alignment as a New Deal Democrat and set him on the road to conservative Republicanism.

In 1964, while all about him in the GOP were losing their

heads, Ronald Reagan became an overnight political superstar, delivering what would later come to be known as "The Speech" to a nationwide television audience. It was a standard litany of conservative virtues and liberal sins, but the phrasing and delivery were better than anything else to come out of the disastrous Goldwater campaign, and they won the fading actor an instant national following that has never abandoned him.

Two years later, an updated version of "The Speech," and the unpopularity of incumbent Democratic Governor Pat Brown (Jerry's father), swept Ronald Reagan into the Governor's mansion in Sacramento and made him the official conservative banner bearer for the GOP.

In retrospect Reagan was a good governor of California— that is to say, a successful one who left his state in better shape than he found it, whether one agrees or disagrees with his rhetoric and specific policies. History shows that even in his failures, he was forward rather than backward looking; in 1973, for example, he supported a tax-limiting proposal that California voters rejected at the time but which proved to be the forerunner of Proposition 13.

Ronald Reagan served two terms as governor of one of the biggest, most complex and turbulent states in the Union and he managed to leave office popular. This was no mean achievement in itself and came as something of a shock to his liberal opponents and the dubious national media—"a surprisingly capable executive who left California in outstanding fiscal condition," as Lynn Rosellini writes.

In 1968 he had been an abortive, unofficial candidate for the presidential nomination. Nixon already had it locked up and the only result of the last minute, improvised effort of some of Reagan's more gung-ho fans was a spirited floor demonstration at the Miami Convention. In 1975, after serving out his second term as governor, he continued piling up political IOUs by touring the country giving fundraising speeches for local GOP candidates. He also kept his name and voice before the public through widely syndicated radio and newspaper commentaries.

Then in 1976, in a tribute to his durability as a popular party figure, Ronald Reagan nearly beat incumbent Jerry Ford for the presidential nomination in his first full-scale attempt at the slot. Ford won on the first ballot, but by an amazingly narrow 1,187 to 1,070 margin, and postconvention bitterness on the part of some Reagan backers may have contributed to Jimmy Carter's squeaker victory over Ford in November.

Reagan himself, despite some snubs from the Ford White House, made at least a token effort to support the GOP ticket and, once the election was over, continued to strengthen his own national base through his radio show, column and speaking tours . . . bringing us up to his decision to run again, which he formally announced on November 13, 1979.

Some of the major positive and negative aspects of both the candidate and his candidacy, can be judged from two of the reactions to Reagan's kickoff address to the nation. On the plus side, conservative columnist James J. Kilpatrick, after looking over the other contenders for the GOP nomination, concluded that

> if Mr. Reagan can maintain the style and pitch and imagery of his opening statement, it is all over but the shouting. His brothers can draw straws to determine who wants to seek second place. This was a class performance. The former California governor projected old ideas in fresh rhetoric, and he advanced a major new idea—for a North American Accord—with grace and boldness.
>
> . . . Mr. Reagan . . . has yet a long way to go. His lack of Washington experience will handicap him sorely in responding to questions about immediately pending issues: windfall profits, welfare reform, changes in tax laws and the like. But he has an able staff and a devoted campaign organization. He presents himself, in Congressman Jack

Kemp's phrase, as the "oldest and wisest." Unless he stumbles, the others will chase his heels in vain.

The speech that "Kilpo" had waxed so enthusiastically about was, indeed, a polished performance—more than a polished performance, since Reagan managed to convey real feeling, especially when addressing some of the social and economic problems facing average Americans. Like all announcement speeches, it was intentionally vague, but it did at least outline some of the overall positions of a Reagan Presidency, notably:

- Cutting taxes as a key to restoring economic health and reviving the private sector.
- Opposing arbitrary growth of government.
- Removal of "government obstacles" [controls and price ceilings, while not specified, are the only things he could have meant] to energy production.
- Support for expanded nuclear power.

This wasn't much, but as political speeches go, at least it was something. Not enough, however, for one of the most influential—and generally conservative—daily papers in the nation. Two days later, the lead editorial in the prestigious *Wall Street Journal* complained of "a speech patently put together by a political packager." The problem, declared the *Journal,* was not Reagan's positions, to the extent that he had taken any.

With only one . . . exception, we agreed with what he had to say. He was for slower growth in federal spending, for lower taxes, for efforts to contain inflation, for a higher defense budget and a stronger foreign policy. What was lacking was any sense that these positions were more than ritual incantations throwing bouquets to various factions in the Reagan constituency. There was no general theme, no sense of priorities—none of the sense of of direction that can come not from staff directors or writers or public opinion polls but only from the candidate himself.

The *Journal* then proceeded to question the practical significance of Reagan's "North American Accord" proposal and his support of statehood for Puerto Rico, the only two specifics in the address, acknowledging that there was nothing wrong with either idea as such, but asking, "What is all this doing as the highlight of a presidential campaign announcement? After all, our whole foreign policy is collapsing around us. The Soviets have military superiority within grasp. The lifelines of Western civilization are in immediate jeopardy in the Persian Gulf . . . ," and so on, in a long list of major problems that did, in retrospect, make the Reagan emphasis seem misplaced if not downright trivial.

"Mr. Reagan," concluded the *Journal,* "was propelled into his position as Republican front-runner by his last campaign, putting heavy emphasis on a more assertive foreign policy and a less obtrusive government."

Time has validated these themes with the electorate. We can understand the political-packaging logic that he can take those votes for granted, and as front-runner should not shake any boats. Though frankly we doubt it, conceivably such tactics will still allow him to slide into the nomination and the presidency. But even if they should, they will have cost him the ability to govern in a way that will make a real difference to the future of this society.

While I happen to agree with the *Journal*'s expressed concern, I can't say that I would have advised Ronald Reagan to do anything other than what he did. As we will see in examining his *Seven Deadly Whims,* he and his team are already at work on a series of complex issue positions that will be unveiled as the campaign progresses. When you're ahead you just don't offer your opponents any targets to snipe at before you have to. And as far as the *nomination* is concerned, Reagan is way out front. As he and his managers see it, their task is to keep the preconvention, intraparty phase of the race as quiet and low-key as possible and to concentrate on strategy and issues that will help Reagan win the general election, most likely matched against Kennedy. Perhaps they're taking too much for granted. But if their reading *is* substantially correct, they are following the right course pragmatically if not idealistically, and helping rather than hindering Reagan's chances of leading a united party into battle in November. Which brings us to Ronald Reagan's *Seven Deadly Whims.*

REAGAN LEADERSHIP (Whim 1)

Reagan's record as governor of California proves that he is capable of leading effectively, at least at the state level. And as California chauvinists are always quick to remind you, running California involves handling much more population, territory and resources—and a bigger gross annual product—than many independent nations can boast. As governor, Reagan's style was relaxed, almost aloof from the day-to-day squabbling of state politics. Yet without ever getting very chummy with the state legislature, Reagan was able to work with it, which is rather the reverse of Jimmy Carter's record in Georgia. Never an obsessive detail man—another difference between himself and Carter—Reagan managed to assemble a solid team of technocrats whose advice he learned to sift, compare and then translate into action where and when he felt necessary. Some of these technocrats and idea men went on to occupy high posts in the federal government, notably Caspar Weinberger who afterwards served with distinction as Secretary of Health, Education and Welfare in the Nixon Administration.

Another trademark of Reagan's leadership as governor was his ability to make real changes—budget cuts, purging of the welfare rolls, major changes in taxes—without polarizing public opinion to a dangerous confrontation level. His calm, affable personality worked as a kind of social balm, and he was able to peacefully advocate and implement policies that, with a raspy leader of the Nixon variety or a more exuberant activist politician like Hubert Humphrey, would probably have engendered endless noise and strife. For all his tendency to speak in clichés, then, Ronald Reagan showed a real leader's sense of balance and ability in choosing advisors and evaluating advice wisely as governor of California.

As a presidential candidate in the past, his record has been less impressive. If being a good governor requires statesmanship, being a good presidential candidate requires political savvy. Reagan, while not devoid of the latter commodity, tends to follow the advice of his campaign advisors almost blindly. This makes him a political manager's dream candidate—putty in the hands of his anointed schedulers, ghostwriters and image makers. But it also means that, if and when his campaign team blunders, he goes over the rail with them. This happened with the disastrous decision to tap Schweiker as his running mate in 1976, and, to a lesser extent, with his automatic endorsement of a controversial, badly researched proposal to cut or transfer responsibility for $90 billion in social programs from federal to state governments that may have cost him crucial early primaries in 1976.

For this reason, even more than with other contenders for the nomination, the calibre of Reagan's campaign organization is vitally important. And as will be seen in Whim 3 (organization) he seems to have done a better job this time around of assembling top-notch issue people.

Still the problem of basic campaign leadership and organization remains—Reagan, as a good-natured but diffident man who doesn't like to rub elbows with the ward heelers, automatically becomes the prisoner of his campaign aides. And they, no matter how talented they are, are then tempted to take more than they should upon themselves. As one long-time Reagan friend and counselor, Lyn Nofziger, complained, shortly after he left the current campaign staff following a series of disagreements with top strategist John Sears: "Everybody always wants to do something their own way with Ronald Reagan and the best way is to just let him talk. Nobody ever figures it out. Each time you gotta go through this whole hassle."

To the extent that Reagan appears to be led around in blinders by his staff, no matter how able they may be, his perceived strength as a leader suffers. And because of his age, people will be looking especially closely for any sign of passiveness, vacillation or simple lack of energy. On the last score at least, Reagan is likely to surprise the skeptics. After all those years sweating under the klieg lights and making grueling tours of the rubber chicken circuit, Reagan at least knows how to pace himself. And old trouper that he is, he tends to pick up energy and enthusiasm as a campaign mounts, invariably finishing more forcefully than he begins.

So, mixed but not hopelessly weak marks for Reagan leadership.

REAGAN COMMUNICATION (Whim 2)

Although there is a strong minority opinion among journalists covering Ronald Reagan that he is lost without notes and can't think on his feet, he is indisputably the finest on-camera performer with a prepared text to run for president in the television era. And despite Senator Bob Dole's acid quip that Reagan doesn't dare give important policy addresses to outdoor audiences on windy days for fear that his file cards might blow away and leave him speechless, he has performed well in a debate format in the past—most notably when he equalled, and in the opinion of many viewers surpassed, William F. Buckley, Jr.—a polished debater if ever there was one—in a

National Public Television debate on the Panama Canal treaties, a technically complicated as well as emotional issue. When he does his homework, Ronald Reagan can think on his feet, which brings us back to the importance of his staff backup in research and policy delineation (Whim 3 again).

As the front-runner for the GOP nomination, Reagan has rightly refused to debate with his rivals, but he has already committed himself to debating the Democratic nominee in the general election campaign. As for stump speaking and structured television spots, he is more than a match for all of the competition in both parties. So high marks as a communicator, with the caveat that the one thing Ronald Reagan needs to communicate more than anything else is the conviction, not currently held by a majority of voters, that he is a truly up-to-date, mainstream candidate rather than an aging 1960s California conservative. It is simply not possible to gauge in advance how deep or insurmountable voter prejudice is on this point, and Republican balloting in primaries and conventions will not necessarily reflect the overall national mood, which will determine events in November. For purposes of winning his party's nomination, however, Reagan leads the field as a communicator.

As for those who accuse him of being repetitious, constantly hammering home the same basic message, the candidate himself has already offered what is probably the best answer. "Isn't it a little bit like a minister?" asks Reagan. "You could say he's saying the same old line—he's got a different sermon every Sunday but his theme is one and the same. My theme, as far back as I can remember, was a warning. . . . The theme is that we continue to centralize authority, we continue with the government growing bigger—and every time we do we're losing freedom."

If that argument doesn't wash with the electorate in 1980, it probably never will, and if Ronald Reagan isn't able to get it across, it's doubtful that anyone can.

REAGAN ORGANIZATION (Whim 3)

One of the most annoying things about modern presidential politics is the way many of the political pundits tend to concentrate on the jockeys rather than the horses. Pick up the morning paper and look at a story ostensibly about Candidate X and, nine times out of ten, the article will spend as much time discussing Candidate X's campaign manager as the candidate himself. For too many political gamesmen, the focus today, to switch metaphors in midstream, is on neither the singer nor the song, but on the songwriter. Of no candidate is this more true than Ronald Reagan. For weeks at a time, if you were to judge by the press clippings, someone named John Sears is running for President and a rather distinguished-looking old gentleman named Reagan is following him around the country, serving as a sort of handy flag of convenience.

This isn't entirely John Sears' fault. He is one of the most brilliant political minds going, and it is only natural that journalists looking for insights into the campaign—and usually denied lengthy interviews with Reagan himself—will fall back on Reagan's strategic mastermind for analysis and augury. He's so damned clever at it—some would say too clever by half.

I first met Sears during Richard Nixon's 1968 campaign when, as an obscure 27-year-old lawyer, he suddenly surfaced as a major tactician in Nixon's dramatic comeback. I was impressed by the quiet, almost monkish Sears then, and I still am today. If he has one fault, I would suggest that he is a little too *much* of a virtuoso. Like a master violinist, he sometimes prefers a flashy, overly complex bravado approach to simplicity and directness. Now that he is in charge of grand strategy rather than tactics, Sears still is obsessed with playing the trick card or springing the novel twist. As one former Sears associate put it in a private conversation with me recently, "The trouble with John is that he doesn't believe there is such as thing as a straight line between two points. And if he did, he'd be bored by it. What he likes to do is weave webs and play games. No one is better at that than John, but he wastes too much time on it."

In 1968 the game playing included squandering a lot of Nixon's man hours and campaign budget on organization and advertising in northeastern states where he never had a chance. Nixon still won, but in a near photo finish with Humphrey and, conceivably, the money and manpower that were poured into lost states like New York and Pennsylvania could have widened Nixon's popular vote margin elsewhere in the country without weakening his electoral vote strength. Again in 1976, Sears attempted, without success, to woo the Northeast for Reagan. And in 1980 he is trying to do it again. "John just can't help himself," his former associate told me. "He looks east to New York the way Mohammedans pray to Mecca. It's something in his blood."

This time, however, there may be some method in Sears' madness. If Regan's hold on Republican support in the South and the West is as strong as Sears believes, then there's no reason in the world why Reagan shouldn't try to cut into his rivals' strength in the Northeast—especially since most of the highly publicized early primaries will take place on the East Coast.

Consider this scenario: If Reagan can win in New Hampshire (and running against a scattered field of opponents he can do so easily just by holding onto a large chunk of the 48 percent of Republican votes he received in the 1976 primary there); if he can make a better than expected minority showing against George Bush in Massachusetts; if he can bury Connally by strong wins in South Carolina and Florida and then carry Illinois, the gateway to the Middle West—then he just might be able to coast all the way to the convention after March 18th.

Sear's hopes to do precisely this by packaging the 1980 Model Ronald Reagan as what he calls a "forward-looking activist." The Sears eastern strategy has produced what *News-*

week magazine has called "a gentle shift centerward" in Reagan's political image if not his stands. "For the first time, a Republican can make the case for positivism, for activism, for progressivism," Sears claims, although some skeptics dismiss the whole package as a case of "cosmeticism."

Whatever this strategy's intrinsic merits, Sears has recruited first-rate talent to produce, direct and field the "New" Reagan. Top-notch teams have been at work for months assembling detailed briefing books on the issues to avoid the kind of damaging slips Reagan made in early 1976. The candidate's Washington policy office is headed by Gary Jones, a former vice president of the American Enterprise Institute (popularly known in the capital as "the conservative Brookings Institute"). Jones is seconded by Agnes Waldron, one of the best researchers in the business, as I can personally attest from several years of experience in the Nixon and Ford White Houses. And Reagan has also received the advice—though not always the endorsements—of leading economic, military and diplomatic experts like former senior presidential economic advisor Alan Greenspan, former Treasury Secretary George Shultz and an array of less famous but respected academic authorities.

Most of Reagan's field operatives are also pretty sound, although as Dave Keene, a senior Reagan campaign aide in 1976 but this year political director for George Bush, puts it, while Reagan has the body count in most states, "you've got to organize it and get it excited, and he hasn't done that." At least he hadn't as of January, 1980. Still, looking at the numbers, the campaign teams and the trends, Keene concedes that if he had to bet on the outcome, he'd still put his money on Reagan—maybe with a longshot side bet on Bush.

Veteran political reporter James Perry seems to agree. After remarking on Reagan's campaign liabilities—overconfidence, some mediocrities in key campaign posts, and an undue reliance on worthless endorsements and tired local party organizations that can't turn out the vote—he quotes Keene as saying that so far the Reagan effort rates only a C-plus.

"But what the candidates trying to overtake Mr. Reagan fear," Perry concludes, "is that a C-plus performance might be enough to win the nomination."

REAGAN WAR CHEST (Whim 4)

Although "Big John" Connally has been by far the most successful early fundraiser in the Republican field (by late November, 1979, he had already netted an estimated $6.6 million, much of it raised by conservative direct-mail fundraiser Richard Viguerie), Ronald Reagan is a proven money magnet who should have no trouble holding his own. In eight months in 1979 alone, he was able to raise $3 million for local Republican candidates on the dinner circuit, and his campaign organization already has a prime list of 400,000 contributors from his 1976 campaign to work with. Besides, in politics the big money always follows a winner. The longer Reagan maintains his clear lead for the nomination, the harder it will be for his outdistanced rivals to raise funds and the more he will automatically attract. High marks for the Reagan War Chest.

REAGAN AGE/HEALTH (Whim 5)

Paradoxically, the oldest candidate in the race is also one of the fittest. Aside from a touch of arthritis in his right thumb, Reagan is in prime condition. His idea of relaxing at his Santa Barbara ranch is setting up fence posts the size of phone poles, a pastime the mere contemplation of which causes a cold perspiration to bespangle the brow of many a suburbanite half his age. His only recurrent health problem is a respiratory pollen allergy—hay fever to the layman. And laboratory tests have proved that the auburn mane that Jerry Ford once described as "prematurely orange" and which another Washington wag has insisted "isn't tinted, it's rusted!" is real and not dyed.

Reagan has also denied that he has had a facelift; journalists who have been given the dubious treat of checking him out behind the ears confirm that he bears no tell-tale operation scars. His blood pressure is a healthy 120/80, and aside from an occasional quavering in his voice, and trembling in his hands, Reagan looks, talks and moves like a man in his late forties or early fifties.

Objectively then, Ronald Reagan deserves high marks for health. But Reagan's age, no matter how good his condition, is an issue that is bound to plague him throughout the campaign. Republican National Committee Chairman Bill Brock is right when he says that if Reagan can make it through thirty-five primary states and capture the nomination, "we'll know that age isn't a problem." At least not a physical one. You can be sure that it will still be an image problem, however, and will loom large in Johnny Carson monologues, in other politicians' statements on their own age and health, and in the minds of many voters in a youth-oriented mass culture.

It is a bald historical fact that Reagan, besides being the oldest man ever elected President, would also be older than almost all first executives were when they retired. Out of thirty-eight past Presidents, three quarters were elected between the ages of 49 and 61. Their average age has been about 54½. So the historic odds, as well as the contemporary mood, would seem to gravitate against Reagan on the age factor, and despite his apparently splendid condition, the best he can hope for on the Age/Health issue is to minimize his losses.

REAGAN MARRIAGE/FAMILY (Whim 6)

Nancy Reagan, says a Reagan supporter who takes what one might call a detached view of his candidate's wife, is an upper-class version of Rosalynn Carter: "She's got the same toughness and fanatical dedication to her husband, but a veneer of good breeding that camouflages it a little." Mrs. Reagan is also more attractive, although there is a coldness in her public smile and her eyes usually seem to be looking past you, at something slightly above and behind your head.

Unlike most political wives, Nancy Reagan is genuinely close to her husband *and* his career—so much so that Reagan occasionally feels the need to tell interviewers that he is not a victim of uxoriousness. He loves Nancy, he will tell you, but he knows his own mind when it comes to politics and can't understand "where the devil this idea" that Nancy calls the shots came from.

"We talk things over," Reagan recently told a visiting interviewer. "It's natural because we are a *we*, we do things together. But that whole attempt to portray her as the ambitious one is not true at all."

Nancy Reagan—at least in front of company—agrees. "Do I have influence over him? Yes. It's impossible to be married that long and not have influence. But as far as sitting back and pulling the strings, no."

What *is* clear is that Nancy Reagan is a strong, intelligent woman from whom her husband derives strength and encouragement—and that alone makes her a definite campaign asset. As governor's lady in California, she had a reputation for a certain remote charm. While she was more popular than not with the general public, Nancy was resented by some local politicians and their wives for preferring wealthy nonpolitical friends and celebrity acquaintances from Reagan's movie past to the rather dowdy politico-social scene in Sacramento. One can hardly blame her.

After twenty-seven years of marriage and sixteen years as political figures, the Reagans remain a loving and secure couple. Their grown children, seldom in the limelight, have never been a source of embarrassing headlines and are unlikely to become so now. And the image of Nancy—trim, immaculately dressed and groomed and always cool and in complete control of herself—is one that most voters would find acceptable if not very exciting. Of all the 1980 candidates' wives, she is easiest on the eyes, and she can give a polished performance when called on to do so. She is also discreet and has no compulsion to be a star in her own right. The only resentment Nancy Reagan is likely to encounter will come from fanatic women's libbers who resent reticent wives and, in the most extreme cases, consider marriage itself a form of institutionalized female slavery. Few of these hags and harridans are likely to vote for Reagan under any circumstances, however, so the net loss is nil.

High marks then for Reagan on Marriage/Family.

REAGAN WILD CARD (Whim 7)

One of the few benefits of Ronald Reagan's advanced age is the unlikelihood of his having any little bimbos stashed away in Burbank or anywhere else. Age aside, after sixteen years of political life, with much of the press and the liberal political establishment digging hard to find any concealed dirty linen, he is not very likely to be faced with any surprise scandals this late in the game.

The only wild cards a man Reagan's age needs to worry about are more likely to involve his private parts than his private life. For example: few things would be more embarrassing or do more to bring home the age issue than Reagan's suddenly having to call a six week time-out from campaigning for a prostate operation. But the older one gets, the more the possibility of that sort of maintenance problem increases. So Reagan must be allotted a negative wild-card rating for possible emergency repairs or debilitating illness sometime between now and November—given his proven stamina and fitness, however, only a small one.

End of whims and time for a few concluding thoughts on Ronald Reagan the man. Robert Benchley once said that it took him fifteen years to discover that he didn't have any talent—and then he couldn't quit because "by that time I was too famous." For over fifteen years his critics have flooded the media marketplace with countless overwhelming reasons why Ronald Reagan shouldn't be taken seriously—first as a political spokesman, then as a governor of the nation's most populous state, and finally as a presidential contender.

Most of the criticism is, in my opinion at least, unfair. But for handicapping purposes, the question is not the validity of such criticism, but how widely it is believed. And the more one looks at opinion samplings of the general public, the more one reluctantly concludes that this aging paladin of the political right has finally come within reach of the Republican nomination a few years and a few campaign seasons too late. Reagan is definitely the front-runner. He will probably be the Republican nominee. But he has a much better than even chance of being defeated in the general election.

In many ways it's a damned shame, for if Reagan does lose it will be for the wrong reasons. His political philosophy, right or wrong, is more popular today than at any time since he first ran for office. But "age-ism" and the feeling that Reagan the politician, like Reagan the film actor, has been in reruns for too long will probably be his undoing—most likely in the general election, but possibly even in the nomination race if his strength in the early primaries erodes and a candidate like George Bush can eliminate the rest of the challengers early and forge a coalition of all the Republican moderates and non-Reagan conservatives.

One is reminded of a particularly heartwarming scene in one of W. C. Fields' films—I believe it was *The Bank Dick*—when the rosey-nosed old reprobate is sharing a morality tale with that priceless nebbish, Grady Sutton. It is the sad story of one of Fields' fictitious uncles, a balloon ascensionist with the unlikely name of Effingham Hoofnagle, who tried to sky-dive into a haystack, failed, and perished in the attempt. "Had he been a younger man," Fields concludes with a sigh, "he might have made it."

Ah well, that's show biz for you . . .

2. JOHN CONNALLY: Talking Tall

The demagogue, whether of the Right or Left,
is, consciously or unconsciously, an undetected
liar.
—Walter Lippmann

HENRY KISSINGER ONCE declared that power is the greatest aphrodisiac. Personally, I question his judgment. To the small degree that I have ever been exposed to the stuff, I've always found it something between an unpleasant distraction from the really worthwhile things in life and a mild soporific. But then writers are strange anyway. If one does take Kissinger at his word—which not everyone is willing to do these days—John Connally must be the randiest candidate in the race. The man exudes power and is a past master at accruing and wielding it. And Herr Doktor Kissinger, whatever his foibles, is a formidable connoisseur of power and ego. Thus his description of John Connally in his recently published memoirs merits consideration as expert testimony:

Highly intelligent, superbly endowed physically, he looked and acted as if he were born to lead [Kissinger writes of Connally]. His build was matched by his ego. His amiable manner never obscured the reality that he would not hesitate to overcome any obstacle to his purposes. "You will be measured in this town," he said to me once, "by the enemies you destroy. The bigger they are, the bigger you will be." John Connally was never afraid of his opponents; he relished combat in defense of his convictions. Whatever one might think of his views, he was a leader.

Without differing from Kissinger's view of Connally as a leader, there are serious reasons for questioning the current wisdom that rates the swaggering Texan as Ronald Reagan's leading challenger. Even the best leader is powerless without followers, and while Connally has managed to assemble a solid campaign command team at the top and has raked in money from the fat cats, he has yet to prove his ability to attract Republican voters *en masse.* It's the old Benedict Arnold syndrome at work again. In 1780, Arnold, one of the most talented of George Washington's generals, switched sides in the Revolutionary War, abandoning his West Point command and joining the British. His defection caused quite a stir at the time, but the British, leery of trusting a turncoat, were afraid to give his talents full play, and so Arnold never again commanded a major army.

Two hundred years later, John Connally, who defected from the Democrats in 1973, has applied for the job of 1980 Republican Commander-in-Chief. And so far, most grassroots Republicans seem to be treating him with the same mixture of awe and distrust that the British did Arnold. Yet the undeniable dynamism of the man is such that large segments of the press, the business community and political professionals think he may be the only man capable of overcoming Ronald Reagan's lead and then beating Teddy Kennedy in a general election.

How much of Connally's strength is real, and how much of it is just a product of the masterful Texan's tall talking? My own reading is that Connally is weaker than he looks and that the same bluster that initially won him headlines and big campaign contributions is starting to cost him votes and esteem—especially among cautious, slightly priggish Republican voters who, on top of everything else, find his speech and mannerisms unpleasantly reminiscent of Lyndon Johnson.

It's only right that they should, for LBJ was John Connally's political godfather. "Big John" cut his political teeth as a young Johnson staffer in the House of Representatives and the Senate in the 1930s and 1940s. It was also Lyndon's patronage as Veep that won Connally his appointment as Secretary of the Navy in 1961—the post that served as his springboard to the governorship of Texas. As Texas governor, Connally proved his own mettle, winning reelection twice and serving three two-year terms from 1963–1969. Tough, articulate and photogenic, John Connally was one of the most popular, successful governors in the state's history. But the fact remains that with the sole exception of George Bush (another Texan and probably Connally's nearest rival), his is the weakest elective record among Republican candidates for the nomination.

Since 1966 John Connally has not been judged by American voters in any contest outside a corporate board room. And he has *never* run in any general election as a Republican. In the ordinary course of events, Connally would still be practicing lucrative law in Houston, as he was in 1971 when Richard Nixon, casting about for a well-known Democrat to take on the thankless post of Secretary of the Treasury—and add a soupçon of bipartisanship to his Administration's economic policy—decided on John Connally.

In 1971, with the Democrats already beginning to set the suicidal course that ended with Nixon's 1972 landslide victory over George McGovern, it seemed as if a drastic political realignment was about to take place. The "Emerging Republican Majority" that Kevin Phillips had prophesied in 1969 seemed imminent, and John Connally decided that he wanted in on the action. So he came to Washington, was an impressive political success as Secretary of the Treasury, went on to head Democrats for Nixon in the 1972 campaign, and, in 1973, formally announced that he had turned Republican.

From then on it was downhill. If John Connally had known in 1973 what he knows now, he would probably still be a Democrat. The new majority died aborning in the rubble of Watergate. And in the prosecution fever that followed, John Connally was indicted and tried on charges of pocketing graft. Washington, which had recently seemed such a warm, promising place, seemed to turn gray around the edges for the high roller from Texas.

It all might have been too much for a weaker man, but John Connally, to his credit, fought back. Exonerated of bribery charges by a full acquittal, he immediately plunged back into politics. Soon he was one of the most popular after dinner speakers on the Republican and corporate lecture circuit. Connally rightly points out that, by being tried and acquitted, he is the only *provenly* innocent candidate in the race. However, like the man who had his head cut off to cure a migraine, Connally may have lost more than he gained. Certainly a residue of scandal still haunts him. The discredited milk-fund charges will be repeated, exaggerated and distorted with increasing frequency if Connally moves up in the race. This isn't fair, but it's routine politics.

Besides his personal magnetism, the two related qualities most often mentioned by Connally's supporters are his pragmatism and his leadership. Unfortunately for Big John, both of these qualities cut two ways, especially among the people most likely to vote in Republican primaries. "Pragmatism"—where strongly ideological Republicans are concerned—smacks seriously of heresy and opportunism. And "leadership" when applied to a glib, somewhat overbearing Texan like Connally summons up unpleasant memories of LBJ. So John Connally's two biggest assets may also prove his two biggest liabilities on the road to the nomination.

And Lyndon Johnson isn't the only albatross hanging around Big John's ruddy neck. In retrospect, he has been singularly unfortunate in his choice of patrons—first LBJ and then Richard Nixon. How well I remember the way Nixon, as President, used to rave about Connally's skill as a political "nutcutter," his powers as a speaker and his ability to "get things done." Several years after Nixon's involuntary retirement, when I spent a few weeks in San Clemente editing portions of his memoirs, the former President was still keen on Connally, considering him head and shoulders above other potential Republican banner bearers. "John's got balls," Nixon declared, once more putting the matter in a nutshell.

In fact it was an open secret back in 1972 that if it hadn't been for grassroots GOP distrust of Connally and residual party loyalty to Spiro Agnew, Big John would have been Nixon's running mate against George McGovern. Had that happened, Connally might be President today.

"Only three men in America understand the use of power," Nixon once told economist Arthur Burns. "I do. John Connally does. And I guess Nelson [Rockefeller] does."

That's quite a tribute until one recalls that "Nelson" understood power so well that he never succeeded in winning the one emblem of power he yearned for more than anything else in the world—the Presidency; and that Nixon, although a skilled power broker in international affairs, misread the domestic power balance so badly that he was, in his own words, hounded out of office because of "a third-rate burglary."

Maybe John Connally is different. He certainly understands the trappings—if not the underlying dynamics—of power. He deserves great credit, to cite but one example, for parlaying little more than his bravado and the dubious prestige of being a retired Democratic governor of Texas to within inches of being Nixon's successor ("Every cabinet should have a future President in it," Nixon told aide John Ehrlichman by way of explaining his appointment of Connally to Treasury—and he meant it).

Connally is definitely, in Arthur Burns' wonderful understatement, "a forceful, ambitious man." But will that be enough to win him the Republican nomination in 1980?

It is widely agreed that John Connally's partisan Republican debut occurred in 1972 while he was still technically a Democrat, heading Democrats for Nixon. His announcement of forming the group, and a subsequent nationally televised speech explaining to Democratic voters why they should vote against McGovern and for Nixon, won him widespread acclaim —and I happen to deserve part of the credit or blame, depending on how you look at it. Thereby hangs a tale that illustrates how often history is made by accident, and how truly pragmatic John Connally can be.

In 1972 I was a White House aide with primary responsibilities as a speechwriter. One morning, without any warning, David Gergen, then assistant to senior presidential writer Ray Price, burst into my office in an obvious state of alarm. I happened to be on the verge of dozing off at the time, having just waded through a particularly tedious sermonette by James Reston in the *New York Times,* but Gergen's sense of urgency quickly brought me to my senses.

"It's the Connally people," he told me. "They liked the kickoff speech you wrote for him, and now they want you to draft a major television address."

"By the way," Dave added on his way out, "they need it by this afternoon."

I lit a cigar, brooded about life's injustice for a few minutes, and tried, as a third generation, East-Coast Republican, to put myself into the boots of a scrappy, ambitious Texas Democrat who had to explain to a hundred million Americans or so why he had defected to Richard Nixon and wanted them to do likewise. Then I started typing. The speech draft reached Connally on time, he used it with only minor changes, and the public reaction was overwhelmingly favorable. It also had a rather funny side effect inside the White House. Bill Safire recounts part of the story in his mammoth memoir of the Nixon years, *Before the Fall.*

> In the 1972 Presidential campaign, the President sent the speechwriters a copy of a Connally speech, with this covering note: "It has the grabbers and the quotable lines. It has no wasted words or high blown rhetoric, but makes all the points. It is high level, hard hitting and simple." We all went up to a screening room to see Connally's speech as he had taped it for television, and the professional admen in the room were stunned by its impact.
>
> "That's some pitch," said one of the image-makers; "who wrote it?"
>
> "Aram Bakshian . . . with a big help from Big Jawn."

Connally's help had come in the form of perfect delivery. We had never met or even talked over the phone, but he had grasped every nuance of my draft, and had given it a masterful reading. Thus, all unbeknownst, I had helped to launch John Connally as a Republican politician.

At the White House, where poor Nixon seldom knew what was going on in the middle and lower echelons, Haldeman tried to use the Connally speech as a club to beat the Nixon speechwriting staff.

"Why is it that Connally's staffers can write zingers like this and *our* people can't?" was the standard snarl until Ray Price finally broke it to one of Haldeman's flunkies that it *was* a White House speechwriter—one A. Bakshian, Jr.— writing hurriedly but free from the usual in-house restraint of bureaucratic editing by committee, who had ghosted Connally's speech.

Mea culpa. Mea maxima culpa.

But enough of tortured trips down memory lane. The point of it all is that John Connally is a quick study, has an instinct for spotting the right line and pitching it to maximum effect, and had most of the supposedly hardboiled political eggs in the Nixon White House, from the President on down, mesmerized. In 1980 he is trying the same number on the Republican Party. So far he has found the going a bit rougher

No one can accuse him of mincing words in the pursuit. John Connally has marked off friendly and enemy constituencies and boldly outlined policies most candidates are afraid to grapple with even in the vaguest terms. He seems to agree with the late General George Patton's approach to battle: "Take calculated risks. That is quite different from being rash."

America—especially American leadership—has gone morally and materially flabby, Connally tells his audiences. We need an unapologetically strong man at the helm again, one who will, among other things:

• Strengthen the fleet, deploy the MX Missile and the Neutron Bomb, and go ahead with the B1 Bomber.
• Balance the budget (which Connally says he would do within two years if elected).
• Cut taxes by as much as $100 billion in the next 3 to 5 years.
• Soften environmental regulations to permit greater use of coal ("The worst environment," he reminds working class audiences, is to be cold, hungry and unemployed . . . it's time to stop taking scientific advice from Jane Fonda and Ralph Nader").
• Speed up the construction of nuclear-power plants.

This little bag of conservative goodies, while more emphatically pitched by Connally, isn't really that different from Reagan's or Bush's preliminary platforms, and, perhaps for that reason, it has been widely ignored by press and public. Where Connally *is* different, and where he has received more publicity than even he may have wanted, is on the ticklish Middle East question. This is the biggest gamble of the biggest gambler in the race, and it seems to have done John Connally more harm than good.

After looking it over and assessing its negative impact on most of the media—and America's affluent and influential Jewish community—I was reminded of a favorite quote from Boswell's life of Doctor Johnson: "That fellow seems to me to possess but one idea, and that is a wrong one." But because it is probably the single most important document to emerge from the early months of the campaign, it seems to me that Connally's nine-point proposal for a peace settlement in the Middle East deserves quoting verbatim, as he first made it in an address to the Washington Press Club on October 11, 1979.

1. Except for minor border rectifications, mutually agreed upon, Israel must withdraw from the West Bank, Gaza and Golan, all of which will be demilitarized. Israel would, however, be permitted to lease military strong points in each of these areas for a mutually agreed upon period of time, and have guaranteed access to these points.

2. All Israeli civilian settlements, including the so-called paramilitary ones, must be withdrawn from the West Bank, Gaza and Golan. The withdrawal should take place on a phased basis, after the peace treaties are signed between Israel and the Arab states, and clear evidence of good faith is established at each stage. Financial assistance for the removal and resettlement of these communities in Israel should be provided.

3. The Palestinian people should decide for themselves whether they prefer the West Bank and Gaza to be governed as an entirely independent entity *or* to be an autonomous area within the Kingdom of Jordan. The

latter approach has great merit and should be thoroughly explored. It would allow the Palestinians to exercise their right to self-determination and self-government within a sovereign Arab state.

Under any arrangement, however, there must be iron-clad provisions barring significant military forces or military relationships which would threaten Israel.

4. Jerusalem's religious significance to Jews, Moslems and Christians, and the city's tragic past, make it an issue of great symbolic importance. No solution will satisfy fully the demands of all the parties. The ultimate resolution of the status of Jerusalem should, however, meet the following criteria:

   (a) Unimpeded access to all the holy places with each under the custodianship of its own faith.

   (b) No barriers dividing the city which would prevent free circulation throughout it.

   (c) Substantial political autonomy for each of the national groups within the city in the area where it predominates.

   The secondary issue of sovereignty over Jerusalem is something that should be considered during the actual peace conference. There are a number of workable alternatives, including Arab or Israeli sovereignty based on residence patterns, a dual sovereignty for the entire municipal region, with individuals deciding which passport they prefer to carry, or possibly some third alternative. Should, after a six-month period, the negotiators remain deadlocked on this issue, the United States should step in to mediate the remaining areas of difference.

5. A customs union between Israel, the Palestinian homeland, and possibly other Arab states should be established as part of the final settlement. This would ensure the free flow of goods and people and integrate the region economically to the advantage of all.

6. A joint Israeli-Palestinian development bank should be

established in Jerusalem. It should be supported proportionally by: (a) the moderate Arab OPEC states, (b) Western Europe, (c) Japan and (d) the United States, all of whom share an intense interest in the Middle East's peace and stability. This bank would have three primary functions:

(a) Contribute to the economic development of the region through the funding of economic infrastructure projects.

(b) Serve as a vehicle to make restitution for lands and property claims which have arisen over the course of the Arab-Israeli conflict. This will include Palestinians who lost land and property as a result of Israeli actions, and Jews who lost land and property in Arab nations as a retaliation. A special international commission would be established to weigh and judge the individual claims.

(c) Act as a financing agent for the relocation of Israeli settlers from the occupied territories, and to assist in the resettlement of the Palestinian refugees.

7. We must secure a clear understanding from Saudi Arabia and other moderate oil producing nations in the region that a just and comprehensive peace settlement means a return to stable oil prices in real terms. The Arabs must, in short, forsake the oil weapon in return for Israel's withdrawal from the occupied territories.

8. The United States should organize a new treaty alliance to cover the Middle East, as a further guarantee of the ultimate settlement, and to protect regional oil fields and shipping lanes from Soviet or terrorist interference. The alliance should include Israel, the moderate Arab states, NATO and Japan. The geostrategic vortex of the struggle between the Free World and Communism has shifted to the Middle East and all of the states with a critical interest in its outcome should bear their fair share of the defense burden.

9. Finally, it should be clear from what I have said that

military and economic stability in the Middle East is a prerequisite to peace, and without greater assurance of military security which translates into the very survival of Israel, the Israelis understandably will not give up the Golan Heights, the West Bank and the military security they provide.

Equally certain, failure to withdraw from occupied territory prevents Israel's antagonists from recognizing the existence, much less the security, of Israel.

No Palestinian self-determination can be achieved under such circumstances, and no reasonable resolution to the status of the holy shrines of Jerusalem will occur except as part of an overall settlement.

As a prelude to peace, who but the United States can provide the political, economic and military stability that will assure time for logic and reason and understanding to overtake and overcome fear, distrust and intransigence?

Therefore, for the critical key that can make a reality of the previous eight points, the United States should maintain a strong military presence in this vital area, including major Air Force components. It may be possible, for example, to lease the former Israeli airfields in the Sinai.

I would propose further that we take elements of the Sixth Fleet in the Mediterranean and the Seventh Fleet in the Far East and, with such augmentation as necessary, create a Fifth Fleet to be stationed in the Indian Ocean.

An immediate approach should be made to the Sultan of Oman with a proposal to develop Masirah Island or another appropriate site into a U.S. naval base to support the new Fifth Fleet and provide security for the Arabian Sea and the strategic Straits of Hormuz.

These steps would demonstrate our determination to further the peace and to protect our other vital interests in the area. Since World War II we have maintained military forces in the Far East and Western Europe for the same purpose. We must now provide a military shield for our Middle East interests as well.

While my own view is that Connally's Middle East bombshell was a political mistake, one has to admire the man for his sheer guts in putting it forward when and as he did. As Rowland Evans and Robert Novak described it in their nationally syndicated political column:

> Connally has offered American voters a serious pre-election formula for Mideast peace. Instead of playing to the important Jewish vote during the campaign, but then turning against Israel from the vantage point of the White House—the customary route of presidential candidates of all persuasions—Connally has borne public witness to his convictions.
>
> Branding him a victim of Arab "blackmail," rather than giving serious attention to what he has proposed, will induce in John Connally this predictable reaction: a national campaign calculated to show that his ideas about America's best interests in the Middle East, far from unique, are shared by many millions of voting Americans.

An interesting possibility, that. Ever since the founding of the state of Israel in 1948 (and Harry Truman's immediate granting of U.S. recognition), it has been a truism of American presidential politics that, whether you're liberal or conservative, Democratic or Republican, you always talk a tough, pro-Israeli line on the way into an election. Connally has not, despite the claims of some of his critics, completely broken with this approach. He recognizes America's indissoluble obligation to the preservation of the Israeli state. But he *has* taken an independent policy line that is at strong variance with Israel's own official policy and that of her strongest partisans in the United States. Within days a predictably shrill reaction had nearly drowned out Connally's original proposal, and his national campaign chairman, former Postmaster General Winton Blount, was complaining that "the Israeli Embassy is orchestrating this campaign against Governor Connally. Apparently they haven't read or do not fully understand the speech."

I leave it to my readers, who have now had the opportunity to read Connally's nine-point proposal themselves, to decide whether it is what he claims or the "total surrender to blackmail by oil-producing countries" that its critics claim. For the purposes of handicapping him as a presidential contender, the real question is whether his position helped or hurt his chances. And that depends in turn on whether or not Republican voters in the primaries are as locked into the traditionally hardline pro-Israeli stance as all of the candidates but Connally seem to think they are. On this question, the *Washington Post* had a surprisingly cool editorial analysis that concluded:

> We suspect . . . that the Connally positions—upholding Israeli security in pretty much the old borders, opening the door to Palestinian moderates while excluding extremists, offering regional military guarantees for reasons of peace and oil alike—represent one possible future wave of American opinion and policy.

The key word, I suspect, is "future." Even if Connally's Mideast stance does represent the wave of the future, I believe that it has damaged his *present* prospects as a nominee and potential candidate—regardless of whether one happens to view him as a prophet without honor or an opportunist betrayed by a poor sense of timing. But we can't be sure until well into the primaries, which makes his Mideast stance one of John Connally's biggest wild cards.

And so to the *Seven Deadly Whims:*

CONNALLY LEADERSHIP (Whim 1)

Strong, not to say pugnacious, Connally may appear to be too much of a leader in the autocratic sense for many voters. Early in the race, while most of his rivals were still struggling to boost their name recognition, Connally's problem was that quite a few people already recognized his name and decided that they didn't like it. My usually calm, scholarly friend, Columnist George Will, who bitterly denounced Big John's Mideast plan, quipped that Connally "may have the support of 80 percent of the officers of the 'Fortune 500' corporations, but they are (to exaggerate just a bit) about 80 percent of his support."

George then illustrated his point with a Field poll taken in California in the spring of 1979, which revealed Connally as the only Republican candidate who "generated more negative than positive impressions," and a more current private poll targeted at Republican primary voters in the Northeast that showed a solid 30 percent "would not vote for Connally under any circumstances." He went on to address the matter of the tall Texan's aggressive campaigning style.

Connally's veiled references to Reagan's age (Reagan is all of six years older than Connally) and Connally's not-at-all veiled references to Chappaquiddick ("I never drowned anybody") are nasty. Perhaps nasty people deserve a candidate, and the nasty constituency is not negligible. Connally may even become "the thinking person's Agnew," which is, of course, a contradiction in terms.

It is this Connally abrasiveness—and the vindictiveness it generates in usually *blasé* commentators like George Will—that raises questions about Connally's leadership image. Some of those sparks of acrimony are bound to kindle voter discomfort—especially among Republican voters already dubious about Connally's party credentials. On the other hand, his tendency to take the clear, hard line where others waffle also sets Connally apart for praise by Americans tired of the usual campaign blahs. On balance then, John Connally is an obviously *strong* leader—but many voters are uncertain whether his is "good" strength or "bad" strength. A mixed rating, therefore, on Whim 1.

CONNALLY COMMUNICATION (Whim 2)

This whim has already been amply discussed in my preliminary observations. Again, it is Connally's harshness that wins some people over at the expense of alienating others—and when you already begin to antagonize large blocs of the public in the first weeks of the nomination race, you have got off to a bad start. Countering the Connally asperity is his outstanding skill as a fist-pounding stump orator. But most voters will not see Connally on the stump. And on television, as an interviewee or scripted performer, Connally, while good, is slightly outclassed by Reagan and about equal to rivals like Baker and Bush. So, again, mixed marks as a communicator.

CONNALLY ORGANIZATION (Whim 3)

There are really two Connally organizations, reflective of his own divided political heritage. The official Connally campaign is run from headquarters in Arlington, Virginia, a suburb of Washington, D.C., headed by Winton Blount and Eddie Mahe. Mahe, who handles the day-to-day details of the campaign and is the senior full-time professional—a crew-cut, chain-smoking veteran of many a Republican war. Since taking on the job, friends say, he has become addicted to Rolaids. Some of his own statements about his candidate help to explain why. "Nobody leads John Connally around by the nose," says Mahe. Big John is "a very, very smart man who has his own opinions and believes in them strongly. His weakness is that he wants to be the campaign manager."

Mahe, who is a former executive director of the Republican

National Committee and a successful campaign consultant, has a skilled staff at his disposal when it isn't being thwarted by unilateral action on Connally's part or by the "other" Connally organization, the tightly organized "Texas Mafia," headed by former LBJ press secretary George Christian and Connally's oldest son, John. There are occasional clashes, but the candidate seems to think they are worth it if they prevent him from being insulated by one small faction in Washington. "The real problem with Nixon," he once told a *Washington Post* interviewer, "was lack of outside advice, the absence of different perspectives that would have made it clear what he had to do." Connally's continued reliance on old friends outside regular GOP ranks will, he believes, keep him free from political tunnel vision.

His pollster, Texan Lance Tarrance, is an experienced political operative who has gained valuable experience at the Republican National Committee and as director of the U.S. census. Hugh O'Neill, an advance man for Ford in 1976, is one of several experienced pros who handle travel, scheduling and media relations.

So as far as individual talent is concerned, Connally is well organized. Some of the early collective results of his team's work, however, have been less than gratifying. In the Florida nonbinding caucuses and convention, for example, Connally was first told by his staff that he might upset Reagan, then that he would finish a very close second and out-distance the rest of the field by a mile. Instead, Reagan finished a very comfortable first with 34.4 percent of the convention votes, while Connally, who had outspent Reagan $300,000 to $225,000 in the state, carried only 26.6 percent, closely trailed by George Bush with 21.1 percent, despite the fact that Bush had only spent $40,000 in Florida and had not mounted a full-scale effort.

But Connally's real test is the early primaries, where actual delegates and massive media coverage are at stake. And here the key, at least as Connally's team sees it, is the South Carolina primary on March 8th. Connally concedes that he will not win in the January 21st Iowa Caucus (and may trail *both* Reagan and Bush). He also admits that he is unlikely to win in New Hampshire and the less important regional primaries in Massachusetts and Vermont.

But he is confident that he will win in South Carolina, where he is counting on open polling in the GOP primary to bring him strong independent and southern Democrat support. On the crest of victory in South Carolina, he then expects to win in Florida, Alabama and Georgia, all of which hold primaries three days later on March 11th. Then, on March 18th comes the big match in Illinois. After Illinois, he says, "we'll know who the Republican nominee will be."

Connally is on record as saying that if he can't "deliver the knockout punch by Illinois," he might as well withdraw from the race.

On the negative side, Connally's strategic reading is sound. He *must* do at least as well as he claims he will in those crucial southern primaries just to stay alive as a serious candidate. Winning most of them *won't* cinch the nomination—it will just keep his campaign afloat. And if Reagan wins big in Illinois, it will probably be all over but the shouting—not only for Big John but for the rest of the challengers as well.

However, Connally's optimism about his potential strength in the South is based on theory and wishful thinking as much as hard facts. No one really knows what will happen in South Carolina, which has never held a Republican primary before and where local experts say that the turnout could vary between 25,000 and 100,000. For this very reason, no matter who wins, the outcome is not likely to offer a really clear reading of party sentiment and should not have much influence on the other southern primaries, especially the crucial race in Florida, where so far Connally's organization has been out-performed not only by Reagan but—considering the modest resources allocated by them so far in Florida—by the Bush forces.

As usual, John Connally is talking tall and doing it rather well —but even if one accepts his own definition of what a successful showing would be (which means discounting early northeastern primaries and exaggerating the importance of South Carolina) Connally's odds for success are still long, which again gives him mixed marks for organization.

CONNALLY WAR CHEST (Whim 4)

No question here. Thanks to Connally's own knack for talking big bucks out of big business, and mass-mail fundraiser Richard Viguerie's expertise at shaking the postal dollar tree, Connally has the strongest war chest of any candidate running for the nomination in 1980. A perfect score for fundraising.

CONNALLY AGE/HEALTH (Whim 5)

Although, as George Will has rather tartly pointed out, John Connally is only six years younger than Ronald Reagan, age is no liability for the strapping Texan. He radiates health, energy, confidence and strength. His only close brush with death came in the fateful Dallas motorcade where he was wounded along with John Kennedy in 1963. His recovery was total, both physically and emotionally. Again, a perfect score for both real and perceived health.

CONNALLY MARRIAGE/FAMILY (Whim 6)

Let me confess at the very beginning: I like Nelly Connally. She is a thoroughly political wife in the best sense—tough, canny and controlled about how much real feeling and opinion she lets show, but she is also obviously devoted to her husband and has the brains, charm and comportment to make a fine First Lady—neither too hoity-toity nor too plebian. She is also a very brave person, as she proved at Dallas in 1963. The surviving Connally children (daughter Kathleen, their fourth child, died in 1959 of what is officially listed as an "accidental shooting," although there were rumors of suicide) are either assets or ciphers—son John will play an active role in the campaign, Mark has a full-time banking career, and daughter Sharon is a housewife with three children. So high marks for marriage/family.

CONNALLY WILD CARD (Whim 7)

Shortly after it became clear that John Connally was a serious candidate for the Republican nomination, a whispering campaign in Washington started spreading the rumor that the closer he got to the nomination, the more damaging conversations on previously undisclosed Watergate tapes would be leaked to the press. So far nothing serious has come out, but the U.S. Archives has barely begun cataloging the 4,500 hours of tapes, a job that is being conducted under maximum security and is expected to take another twenty months to complete at the earliest. Connally insists that there is "not a thing" on the tapes that could possibly damage him, but one can never be sure, and their very existence—especially given the past record of leaks where Watergate evidence was concerned —injects at least a modest negative wild-card factor. Connally's acquittal on charges of accepting $10,000 from milk producers while Secretary of Treasury legally closes the books on graft allegations, but inevitably, the aroma will linger with some dubious voters. All in all then, Connally, with his whiff of scandal and his controversial Mideast stand, comes up with the most negative wild-card rating next to Teddy Kennedy—although his problem is of nowhere near the same proportions.

So much for whimsy. Before moving on to George Bush, a few closing thoughts on Big John as both a candidate and a potential President. My own feelings about the man are very ambivalent. To put it as plainly as possible, I believe he is running a high-risk campaign and would prove to be a high-risk/high-yield President if nominated and elected. He is a true patriot but also a true autocrat in the LBJ mold—more polished than Lyndon but every bit as overbearing and egotistical. That is why so many voters fear him—and so many others see him as the only man strong enough to deal with the current national mess. From a writer's point of view, a Connally Presidency would be fascinating and fun. Watching him swing into action always is. But I believe that in 1980, the people he frightens—and the people in whom he inspires distrust or distaste—will outnumber his supporters in the GOP race.

If he could get through that, he would probably beat Carter and would at least give Kennedy a blistering run for his money. But it just isn't in the cards for 1980—at least as I read them.

And having reached that conclusion, even as the cautious citizen in me breathes a sigh of relief, my historian's appetite for color and the political voyeur streak that is a part of any Washington insider's pschological makeup feel a real sense of disappointment.

What a show it could have been. And may yet be; for to borrow a thought from Jerry Brown, in 1984 Big John Connally will still be younger than Ronald Reagan is today.

Hang in there, Big Brother.

3. GEORGE BUSH:
Politician as Preppy

Spurn not the nobly born
With love affected,
Nor treat with virtuous scorn
The well-connected.
High rank involves no shame—
We boast an equal claim
With him of humble name
To be respected!
—*Sir W. S. Gilbert,* Iolanthe

IN AN AGE of inverted snobbery, the
rise of George Bush on the political scene is a reverse Horatio
Alger saga—a quirky modern success story that could only
happen in America. George Bush is living proof that with luck,
pluck and elbow grease, a well-bred New England WASP can
survive the fine-grinding mill of education at Greenwich
Country Day School, Phillips Andover Academy and Yale, live
down the excruciatingly fey nickname of "Poppy," and slowly
but surely ascend the tawdry ladder of American politics.

Few of his contemporaries on the election scene have had
to overcome such heavy odds just to make it to the starting
gate. Lesser spirits would have quailed at the mere prospect.
But George Bush, at 55, has somehow managed to live down
the unfortunate accident of his high birth, the damning taint
of being a scion of what the late P. G. Wodehouse once de-

scribed as, "the best people—cultured men accustomed to mingling with basset hounds and women in tailored suits who look like horses."

It cannot have been easy, but adversity has ever been the handmaiden of greatness, and one suspects that the bard Tennyson, in one of those moments of prophetic insight nature sometimes grants great artists, had "Poppy" Bush in mind when he strummed his lyre and gave voice to the heroic sentiment:

> And thus he bore without abuse
> The grand old name of gentleman,
> Defamed by every charlatan,
> And soiled with all ignoble use.

Bravo, Poppy! So sanguine has his achievement been that today, if anyone is capable of stopping Ronald Reagan on the way to the GOP convention in Detroit, it is probably Bush. The problem he overcame along the way is not altogether new; Aristophanes, writing at the height of ancient Athenian democracy, noted that the characteristics of the typical popular politician were "a horrible voice, bad breeding, and a vulgar manner"—all things that cruel nature denied George Bush. But he managed to succeed without them. Nobly done, blue-blooded Bush: You may be the first true American aristocrat to mount a serious race for the Presidency since Franklin Roosevelt—and he doesn't really count since, as a few of the more doddering members of the Manhattan Harvard Club can still be heard to mutter over their port, FDR was a "traitor to his class."

Not George Bush. Far from turning his back on the ancestral roots, he merely allowed them to grow beyond the old Yankee confines to embrace a larger chunk of America. Where a more complacent man in his position would have found it all too easy to feather his nest in New England, playing a muted role in the genteelly crumbling local GOP establishment (which, as the son of Connecticut Senator Prescott Bush's widow, he could have taken for granted), young George headed west.

And thus it came about that Bush, armed only with his economics degree from Yale (and perhaps a dab of pocket money to ante up with) found himself in Texas. After five years of apprenticeship with an oil company, he founded the Zapata Petroleum Corporation in 1953 and, as its president and chairman from 1956–1966, turned it into a thriving multimillion dollar operation.

Money isn't everything, and having proven that he was his own man as a manager and entrepreneur, George Bush was soon making a name for himself in Texas politics as well. In 1964, when Barry Goldwater's presidential candidacy was simultaneously crippling the GOP in the rest of the country and bringing in new recruits in the South and parts of the Southwest, George Bush ran for the Senate in Texas. It was the wrong year in the wrong state; a Texan by the name of Johnson was at the head of the Democratic national ticket and George Bush was one of his first casualties. But in 1966 Bush bounced back, capturing a newly-apportioned House seat in southwest Houston. He served two quietly distinguished terms in the Congress, during which he made a favorable impression on many of his colleagues—including then minority leader Gerald Ford, who ten years later would call on Bush when he needed a man he could trust to take over the ruins of the CIA in the aftermath of Watergate.

My own first encounters with George Bush took place while he was still a congressman. The impression I had of him then has changed remarkably little in the intervening dozen years. I particularly remember Bush as one of the more pleasant, intelligent and purposeful members of a GOP congressional task force on campus conditions that Representative Bill Brock of Tennessee (now Chairman of the Republican National Committee) organized with some of the brighter young GOP

House members in 1969. The purpose of the group was to meet face-to-face with students, faculty and administrators at every kind of American institution of higher learning, without the glare of publicity, and try to come to grips with some of the basic sources of student frustrations. As staff director of this well-intended if not very earth-shattering effort, it fell to me to deal with and occasionally massage the twenty-two congressional egos involved, most of them sure that they, and they alone, knew all the answers.

They were a rather contrasting bunch, including such colorful characters as Don Riegle, who afterwards switched parties and is now a Democratic Senator from Michigan; maverick ex-marine Pete McCloskey, an outspoken but more likable member of the group's left wing; a somber Baptist preacher-turned-politician from Alabama named Buchanan; the late and much-lamented Bill Steiger of Wisconsin (then one of the youngest and most promising members of Congress); and an assortment of lesser characters. George Bush stood out from the crowd for his affability and crisp but never brusque purposefulness, and his sound, *sanely* conservative views. He was also efficient, well-organized and considerate of others—not a set of qualities one often finds combined in a single congressman.

It has been ten years now since George Bush left the House of Representatives to make a second unsuccessful run for the Senate in Texas—a defeat that was largely due to one John Connally's activities on behalf of the Democratic candidate, Lloyd Bentsen (who is now, rather amusingly, being talked about as a possible running mate for Teddy Kennedy—something "Big John" could hardly have foreseen back in '70 when he helped launch Bentsen as a senator). Except for that second Senate defeat, it has been a positively eventful decade for George Bush, though he shows few signs of wear.

Meeting him recently during a visit at the American Enterprise Institute in Washington, I was struck by how little he had aged physically since the late 1960s when I had first met and worked with him. He was still tall, trim and youthful in bearing, and except for a little more gray in his hair he hadn't aged a bit. And yet since then he had served as U.S. ambassador to the United Nations from 1971 to 1973, as chairman of the Republican National Committee from 1973 to 1974, as first chief of the United States liaison office in Peking from 1974 to 1975, and as director of the CIA from 1976 to 1977.

Since then he has spent most of his time running for President, steadily gaining ground on rivals with far greater name recognition, and he has managed, man for man, to assemble what is probably the most efficient campaign organization in the field—although still considerably smaller in scale than Reagan's and not as lushly funded as Connally's.

In the months before the first primaries, George Bush made good use of this organization; he was the *only* candidate who consistently did better than expected against the other contenders for second place in the race—John Connally and Howard Baker. Bush and his strategists have repeatedly demonstrated the best sense of timing and priorities in pacing and targeting objectives—first concentrating on building up organizational strength in Iowa, New England and Florida, and then steadily fanning out from a tightly-knit base while circulating the candidate among key interest groups and local leadership. Rather than squandering early resources on a costly and premature communications blitz to make George Bush a household name among the large mass of voters who will not even participate in the nominating process, Bush and his managers concentrated on meeting with and recruiting from the relatively small cadre of GOP activists, and winning local exposure for the candidate in target areas of key primary and caucus states.

It was a big job, but by the end of 1979 George Bush had already logged half a million miles of travel and visited thirty-eight states without showing any signs of tiring. And, initially at least, his strategy had paid off with straw-vote victories in Iowa, a nonbinding caucus win over Howard Baker in Maine, and an unexpectedly strong showing behind Reagan and Connally at the nonbinding Florida GOP convention. As Campaign 1980 began in earnest, George Bush was even beginning to be taken seriously by the Washington press corps—invariably the last people to get word of news from the front.

If nominations, like wars, are usually won by those who have learned the most from the last conflict, then George Bush has a good chance of surprising more than the Washington press corps. By the end of 1979, savvy political correspondents like David Broder were coming to realize that "Bush has made better use of 1979 than any of his rivals," and that "like Carter [in 1976] he has used living-room meetings, where he, his wife or one of his sons has been present, to build a network of volunteers whose commitment is not lessened by the fact that most of them knew nothing of George Bush when 1979 began."

After the Florida convention, as *Post-Newsweek* columnist George Will observed before, "Connally insisted that the Republican race is a two-man race between him and Reagan, because only he can beat Reagan. My hunch is that the race may be, indeed, closer than most people think to becoming a two-man race, but that the two men are Reagan and Bush."

John Sears, who earlier had blithely insisted that the only entries Reagan had to worry about were Connally and Baker, was also having second thoughts. As for the Baker camp—disillusioned and demoralized by staff shakeups and their candidate's chronic neglect of serious campaign planning—several key organizers told me privately in late November of 1979 that if things didn't shape up before the end of the year, they would probably bolt to Bush and take their local troops with them. Meanwhile, John Connally's chairman in Iowa, David Readinger, was actually predicting that besides leading Connally, George Bush might actually beat out Reagan in the January 21st caucuses—the first real test of strength in the race, and the vehicle that transformed an obscure ex-Governor of Georgia from "Jimmy Who?" to the hottest media star of the race in 1976.

Like Bush, Carter entered Iowa with incredibly puny name recognition and minuscule support in the opinion polls against a field of much better known candidates and potential candidates. But once Carter outperformed his rivals in Iowa, he got all of the media exposure he needed to bridge the name-recognition gap and simultaneously garnered the favorable image of an underdog turned winner—just the kind of political Cinderella story that appeals to the popular (or at least the journalistic) imagination.

To get the same benefits, Bush doesn't even have to beat Reagan in Iowa—so long as he runs a close second. The closer he comes the more easily he can parlay his Iowa showing into the big coverage and building public momentum he needs to eliminate serious third candidates like Baker and Connally early in the race.

Unquestionably, then, George Bush has to be taken seriously —much more seriously than his fellow candidates and the media realized at the beginning of the marathon race for the nomination. But how does he shape up against Bakshian's *Seven Deadly Whims?*

BUSH LEADERSHIP (Whim 1)

As a businessman, as a student, as a carrier pilot during World War II, as a congressman and as a senior functionary in intelligence, party and diplomatic posts, George Bush has shown that he can lead and has won the admiration of observers and the loyalty of his subordinates. With an estimated worth of between $1.6 and $1.7 million, he can truthfully say, "I did not inherit a lot of money. I left the East and went down to Texas and built a business and *made* what money I've got."

A former employee, oil-drilling consultant Carl Johnson, Sr., remembers Bush as "very cool in a crisis operation. He takes time to think it out before he goes about whatever has to be done . . . fair, a good man who's worked hard all his life."

Bush volunteered for the Navy Reserves immediately after graduating from prep school and was commissioned as a pilot at eighteen, the youngest in the service. His war record, while he treats it lightly, was a distinguished one: "I was shot down in the Pacific at age twenty. I'm not sure that's the best credential for a presidential candidate, but that was my first governmental job and it imbued in me the ideal of service," he told political reporter James Dickenson in an interview late in 1979.

Representative Barber Conable, a veteran Republican legislator from New York, got to know Bush well during his two terms as a Texas congressman. "I know George is a long shot," concedes Conable, who is a member of the Bush campaign steering committee, "but I believe in him. . . . He has a good deal of support in Congress. . . . George's personality is a youthful one. . . . He hasn't burned out his youthful idealism."

Those who worked with Bush at the United Nations and the Republican National Committee also give him high marks for brains and energy—and for a persistence that sometimes borders on stubbornness. Temperamentally, they say he is generally outgoing and relaxed. Although he has been known to lose his temper over staff blunders and has a reputation for not suffering fools gladly, he is not one to hold grudges.

Senator Daniel Inouye of Hawaii, the Democrat who chairs the Senate Select Committee on Intelligence, says that George Bush was "one of the best CIA directors we've had," and—unique among recent heads of the agency—he seems to have left the job unstained and unscarred.

All this denotes real leadership. But what about perceived leadership and the more specialized leadership skills required of a candidate for the Presidency? Bush has already proven that he can attract and select a good staff and a good core bloc of committed supporters. However, his two defeats as a candidate for statewide office in Texas, and the absence of any positive elective track record beyond his two terms as a congressman from Houston, raise some doubts about George Bush's proficiency as a *seeker* of high office if not as a holder of same. As a political leader—a candidate—Bush remains an unproven quantity, and to a large if contracting chunk of the electorate he is still "George Who?"

So mixed but basically positive marks for Bush's leadership.

BUSH COMMUNICATION (Whim 2)

George Bush is not a spellbinder on the stump, but he's a much better speaker today than when he entered the race. In my characterization of him as a man who had gone a long way to overcome the political disadvantages of good breeding, I particularly had in mind the way Bush—after some months of modest, self-effacing speeches that were the despair of his campaign aides—buckled down to a crash course in communications. For several weeks he spent three hours a day practicing a more assertive—Aristophanes would, I suppose, have called it ill-bred—speaking style. The gestures gradually became more forceful, more emphatic. He finally discarded the rather goofish pair of "granny glasses" that his wife, Barbara, had been urging him to scrap for years, and generally tightened up his communications style.

"What have they done," an amazed Reagan supporter asked me after he watched the "new" George Bush roll triumphantly through his first posttraining television interview in the fall of 1979, "given him hormone injections or something?"

Washington Post reporter Bill Peterson commented on the difference a few weeks later:

Months ago, Bush's friends, like Mac Baldridge, his Connecticut chairman, told the candidate that if he expected them to work their tails off for him he would have to get more forceful, not another John Connally, but less like a professor lecturing the Council on Foreign Relations.

Most politicans I have known over the years would not have taken kindly to such advice. They would resent it either because they already considered themselves polished speakers, or because their egos were too frail. Bush paid attention, hired a voice coach, took a critical look at himself, and became, in Peterson's words, "more confident and more strident." While some of the press find the new Bush style "unnatural and strained," the overall reaction is favorable. In comparison to his major rivals, I would rank the "new" Bush—the only one most voters will ever see—as at least a match for Howard Baker as both a formal speaker and an impromptu debater and interviewee; equal to Reagan and only slightly behind Connally in the impromptu department; and still outgunned by Reagan and Connally on the stump working with a script. He is the peer or superior to all of them at actually mingling with the public and working a crowd, whether at a factory gate or in a country-club cocktail lounge. "He actually seems to enjoy the grind," *Time* magazine correspondent John Stacks has observed with something close to amazement, "maintaining a good humor, bantering easily with aides and joking about some of the absurdities in politics."

Again the mixture of stamina and a sense of balance is as refreshing as it is rare—most candidates tending either to be mindless extroverts or loners with good brains who must be coaxed or shoved into any contact with the public.

One of George Bush's most striking communication strengths is harder to define and quantify. The candidate's political director, Dave Keene, touches on it when he speaks of Bush's "cultural background [that] makes him acceptable to moderates and the establishment," at the same time that his issue positions are those of a firm conservative. For once, Bush's patrician background is a boon—it makes him respectable in political and media circles where most candidates with his views encounter raised eyebrows and wrinkled noses. The old school tie is still good for something after all; it gives George Bush the positive aura of a "moderate" among moderates without undercutting his standing as a conservative among conservatives.

Bush was one of the first to realize this advantage. Way back in July of 1979 he was already predicting an ideological and stylistic process of elimination that would end with him as the Republican nominee. What he visualized, he told political reporter James Perry, was a kind of image scenario in which voters would gradually perceive Reagan as too "old," Connally as too "slippery," Bob Dole as too "mean," John Anderson as too "liberal" and Phil Crane as too "conservative." This would leave the field to Bush and Howard Baker—a case of the most moderate conservative versus the most conservative moderate. And so far, at every turn in the road, Baker, despite a stronger popularity rating in the opinion polls, has been outmaneuvered by Bush.

BUSH ORGANIZATION (Whim 3)

More than any of his rivals, Bush has been able to recruit some of the most talented organizers from all wings of Republican politics. The Bush campaign is a Republican ecumenical movement—largely because of his ability, just discussed, to impress moderates with his cosmopolitan image while maintaining *bona fides* as an ideological conservative. The Bush staff list is not as long as Reagan's or Connally's, but it is stronger on individual talent:

• Campaign chief Jim Baker, a prominent Houston lawyer, was the respected head of the Ford campaign in 1976.

• Political director Dave Keene, a senior Reagan aide in 1976, is one of the sharpest political minds in the business.
• Finance chairman Robert Mosbacher, a millionaire yachtsman, headed Ford's successful fundraising effort in 1976.
• Press secretaries Pete Teeley and Susan Morrison are both top political pros—Teeley, a former aide to the Republican National Committee, the 1976 Ford campaign and New York Senator Jacob Javits; Morrison, an active flack in national *Democratic* politics.
• Pollster Bob Teeter is probably the most widely used and respected opinion sampler in Republican politics.
• Speechwriters and issues advisors include such heavyweights as economists Herb Stein and Arthur Burns, former National Security Council boss Brent Scowcroft, veteran GOP power broker Dean Burch and former Nixon and Ford speechwriter Dave Gergen.

The high caliber of Bush's national organization is reflected at the state and local levels. *Wall Street Journal* reporter James Perry, in an excellent nuts-and-bolts account of modern nomination politics, describes how Bush's Iowa organization was born.

On a cold winter night last February [1979], six young Iowa Republicans met at the home of Ralph Brown in Dallas Center, a 45-minute drive west of here, to talk about Presidential politics.
    'We agreed that night,' says George Wittgraf, a Cherokee, Iowa, attorney, 'that Ford wasn't viable . . . and that Reagan was too old. What we began looking for was someone to bridge the gap between the moderates and the conservatives so we could avoid the kind of nasty split we had in 1976.'

Looking around, the group decided on George Bush because of his distinguished public service, his party credentials and his image. So they formed the nucleus of what grew into a crack state organization with individual coordinators in most of Iowa's ninety-nine counties, a budget of nearly $300,000 and a full-time professional staff of ten.

Where Bob Collins, Reagan's Iowa campaign manager, is relying on the old-fashioned, broad-brush approach, planning to use volunteers to telephone all 200,000 Republican households in the state, Wittgraf's approach is more professional: "There are at least 600,000 people in Iowa who identify themselves as Republicans. But no more than 30,000—40,000 tops—will participate in the caucuses. When you get right down to it, the really active Republicans in this state are a hard shell of maybe 5,000 people. The winner in these caucuses could be the fellow who gets 7,500 votes."

Two months before the caucuses, the Iowa Bush organizers had already lined up 2,300 firmly committed supporters pledged to participate in the caucusing—a full quarter of the support they think they'll need to win. If Bush does win in Iowa, it will be a classic example of the triumph of fine-honed micropolitics over conventional macropolitics.

"Sure you can make fun of this system as being a strange way to nominate a President," Wittgraf told the *Wall Street Journal*'s Perry, "but in Iowa we'll have thought pretty hard about it. I estimate George Bush will have met 10,000 Iowans by the time it's over, and those people will know something about him. I think 30,000 or 40,000 Iowans who go out on what probably will be a cold, dark night in January are as capable of making these judgments as any other Americans."

BUSH WAR CHEST (Whim 4)

Bush began 1980 with rising prospects that should keep the money flowing in, especially if he can perform up to expectations in Iowa caucusing and the early primaries. By late 1979 he had already raised approximately $3.5 million, running a comfortable third to Reagan and Connally, in that order. His campaign is well financed and—equally important—seems to be getting better mileage out of its money than all the rest. High marks on War Chest.

BUSH AGE/HEALTH (Whim 5)

At 55 George Bush is a jogger who doesn't collapse. More than one flabby member of the fourth estate has had to conk out in midinterview while the 6-foot-3, 190-pound candidate continued to lope easily down a New Hampshire or Iowa road at 6 A.M. in the morning. An avid sportsman who plays aggressive games of basketball, golf, badminton (you can be sure he doesn't emphasize that one with blue-collar audiences) and tennis, George Bush is in excellent physical condition and, more importantly for political purposes, looks it. A perfect score on Age/Health.

BUSH MARRIAGE/FAMILY (Whim 6)

Barbara Bush is probably the most intelligent, relaxed contender for First Lady in the Republican column. Her marriage is clearly a happy one, and the couple—after 34 years, five children and two grandchildren—still seem to really share their public and private lives. Mrs. Bush, tanned and white haired, looks a bit more matronly than one might expect on first meeting, but she has a gracious, open manner, a sense of humor and an easy self-confidence that puts the visitor at ease. She isn't too nervous to joke, even about her husband. When he told an interviewer from the *Christian Science Monitor* that he liked country-western music and his favorite dish was barbecued ribs, Mrs. Bush's quick aside was, "There goes your image." Their children are clean, bright and articulate—two of the sons are campaigning for their father full-time. Barbara Bush is also working the hustings with good results. She is an asset on the campaign trail and would make a fine First Lady. Top marks on Marriage/Family.

BUSH WILD CARD (Whim 7)

On the negative side, George Bush has two things going against him. A number—uncertain but not negligible—of rightists in the Republican Party have a real obsession about the legendary Trilateral Commission and, to a lesser extent, the Council on Foreign Relations, both "Eastern Establishment" organizations Bush has belonged to. He resigned from both in September of 1978, at about the same time he started seriously considering running for the presidency. But a lingering paranoia abides. What the Freemasons used to be to credulous Catholics, and the "Night Doctors" to superstitious Blacks, the Trilateral Commission is to the rabid Right—a sinister conspiracy involving Gnomes of Zurich, Elders of Zion, and oodles of Rockefellers. This is hardly a matter of concern to the general electorate, but it could be a negative factor for Bush if Reagan's hard right strength begins to crumble and some of it shies away from Bush because of these severed organizational links. John Connally, for one, considers it a major Bush handicap and has said so publicly.

At the other end of the spectrum there are some voters, equally paranoid but in the other direction, who will probably never forgive George Bush for being a director of the CIA. Most of this gang wears red rather than white tennis shoes and vote in Democratic rather than Republican primaries. Bush probably never had their support—he certainly won't lose it to Ronald Reagan or John Connally.

Politically and personally, Bush seems to be fairly scandal proof. Anyone who could ride out the post-Watergate storm as head of the CIA without incurring even minor smudges must be pretty clean. As for his private wealth, Bush, an early champion of full disclosure as a congressman, has already voluntarily made his financial records public. On the intimate personal level, even in salacious Washington, where hanging out dirty linen is a minor industry, one has yet to hear the first nasty rumor about George Bush. Scout's Honor.

So George Bush does rather well on the *Seven Deadly Whims*. He has few if any built-in weaknesses in his candidacy and plenty of potential for growth. In my personal view, he is the most promising Reagan challenger—with the understanding that, as dear old Senator Everett Dirksen, the beloved "Wizard of Ooze," told me years ago, "People don't win elections. Their opponents lose them." Reagan must stumble before Bush can really get into gear. Until then, all George Bush or any of the other challengers can hope to do is cannibalize each other.

Beyond the nomination, I see Bush as a plausible, positive candidate in the general election. I also believe he is better qualified than most of his rivals to actually *be* President. I trust both his intellect and his instincts, and I believe that while implementing a fairly conservative program for the nation, he could still maintain his credibility with Blacks, other minorities and Democrats in the Congress. I remember one of the toughest decisions Bush had to make when he was in Congress. He risked his popularity in Texas to take a stand for human dignity by voting for open-housing legislation, knowing even as he did so that he would lose many white votes without gaining any significant strength among Blacks and Chicanos. That, says George Bush in retrospect, "was not a liberal or conservative vote. I thought it was a fair-play issue."

Not bad, Poppy—in fact, downright presidential.

4. HOWARD BAKER: Tennessee Stalking Horse

*. . . dull disposition, lukewarmness and sloth,
are not seldom wont to cloak themselves under the
affected name of moderation.*
—John Milton

VIEWING THE REPUBLICAN field with the donnish humor of a trained academician who also happens to be a syndicated political columnist, Jeffrey Hart suggested that "if you could fuse . . . Baker and Bush into one candidate, a Bakerbush, you might have something to work with. . . . As of now, Baker has good polls and no organization. . . . Bush is just the opposite. He has been organizing well in Iowa, New Hampshire and elsewhere, but you would need an electronic microscope to find his popular support."

Up to a point, Lord Copper. My only proviso to this analysis would be that early in the race, organizational strength is much more important than general popularity. With good organization, an attractive but obscure candidate can quickly build popularity; without good organization, a candidate with broad but unfocused popularity may never get off the ground

—at best he'll have a hard time translating it into demonstrable strength in low-turnout caucuses and primaries. Not to mince words, if—God forbid—I were ever mad enough to run for President, I would much rather start the race in George Bush's shoes than Howard Baker's.

Merit has little to do with it. Having observed Howard Baker's Washington career from the start (I was an aide to a Tennessee congressman when Baker won his first election in the Volunteer State in 1966), I am convinced of his high intelligence and parliamentary skill. I believe that he would make an effective presidential candidate in the 1980 general election, and I am even more confident that if elected he would prove a trustworthy and competent first executive. But there's more to it than that. Baker, writes Jeff Hart,

> can argue plausibly that he has been an effective minority leader in the Senate. As he likes to put it, he has kept both Jacob Javits and Barry Goldwater on the same team. A typical border state politician, and an intelligent political pro, Baker has been an effective negotiator and compromiser. . . . His liabilities are also glaring. Baker needs to overcome the impression that he is the Thomas E. Dewey of 1980—the smooth tactician who "speaks well" but who really stands for little and arouses no passion. As it was put in 1948, Dewey was like the little doll-bridegroom on a wedding cake, plastic, and, when you get right down to it, boring.

Reflecting on Baker's formal announcement as a candidate, columnist George Will recalled that when *Newsweek*'s Capitol Hill staff canvassed Democratic senators' presidential preferences in 1978, they came away with the impression that a majority of the Senate's Democrats would be happy to see Minority Leader Howard Baker the next President—no mean bi-partisan vote of confidence. As Will concluded, "The Sen-

ate, a grave of many reputations, has been good for Baker's."
But alas, Democratic senators do not vote in Republican primaries. It's the Howard Baker paradox in microcosm—the
very qualities that make him a successful legislator and would
probably make him an effective President count for little, or
actually undermine his strength as a candidate for the Republican nomination. All the world loves a moderate if one believes
the polls, but all the world has little to say about who will be
selected by the GOP at its 1980 convention in Detroit. And
Baker's immoderate pursuit of moderation has clearly not won
him the enthusiastic loyalty of a solid professional network of
organized party operatives, despite a public popularity running second only to Reagan among Republican and independent voters in many polls, which also give Baker the lowest
negative rating among major GOP candidates.

Extremism in the pursuit of moderation may be no vice, but
in his attempt to cut out his territory as the leading party
moderate, Howard Baker may have gone a little too far for
some rarefied Republican tastes. As one bemused non-Baker
party activist said to me after watching the Tennessean deliver
one of his typically low-key, balanced speeches, "If Howard
gets the nomination this time, they'll have to take the old
Goldwater slogan out of mothballs and 'modify' it for him.
Remember how it went in '64? 'In Your Heart You Know He's
Right.' For Howard it'd have to be, 'In Your Gland You Know
He's Bland.'"

Baker himself is so insatiable in the cultivation of his neutral
image that he even describes himself as being only "moderately" religious. Granted that Jimmy Carter has given pious
politicians a bad name, this still seems a bit much, especially
for an East Tennessee Presbyterian—rather like claiming to be
half a virgin.

A more objective problem plaguing what could be a promising candidacy is Howard Baker's seeming inability to recruit
and utilize an adequate campaign team. As a senator he has

always had a personal reputation for brains—but the collective gray matter of Baker's Senate staff has never been highly esteemed by political insiders.

As long as he was only a senator, it really didn't matter. With a secure popular base in his home state, Howard Baker hasn't needed that much of a high-powered staff in the past. He does most of his own thinking on policy and can rely on men and women of modest attainments to handle mundane matters like servicing the local Tennessee media, doing casework and dispensing routine patronage.

Running for President is different. Baker's poor staff record was one of the main reasons why—to my certain personal knowledge—at least two very prominent national Republicans with strong Tennessee ties flatly refused to head Baker's campaign organization despite the urgent personal invitation of the candidate. As for Baker, although he has chopped off a few heads and shifted a few appointments in the wake of early campaign miscarriages, he still doesn't seem to realize the gravity of his problem—or simply won't admit to himself how important a factor organization is. He remains aloof, ignoring concerned advisors and allowing his campaign effort to drift.

In this he is not alone, particularly among his Senate colleagues. There is something about the pampered, complacent atmosphere of the Senate Chamber that insulates many of its most able inmates from the realities of nuts-and-bolts nomination politics. They seem to feel that by being good senators they will automatically attract the necessary national presidential support and can therefore afford to leave the practical side of the campaign to a few loosely supervised boys in the backroom. It just doesn't work that way anymore. If it did, Edmund Muskie or Scoop Jackson might be President today—and the country might be considerably better governed than it has been under Jimmy Carter.

But more of these organizational ills when we get to Howard

Baker's *Seven Deadly Whims.* First let's take a brief look at the man's personal and political roots.

To understand Howard Baker, it helps to know a little about the part of Tennessee he hails from. Baker was born in Huntsville, Tennessee (population: 387) on November 15, 1925, an heir to the local squirearchy. He comes from a long line of officeholders, including a father and stepmother who both were members of Congress. Huntsville is in mountainous East Tennessee where moonshining is still the major crime problem and the local folk—in clear contradistinction to the majority of Tennesseans living in the middle and western areas of the state—have been loyal Republicans ever since Civil War days. In East Tennessee, the GOP is literally the party of Lincoln, its loyalty forged by bloody ties that go back to the Civil War. Mountaineers, an old Latin proverb has it, are always free men. Perhaps this is what impelled the tough, marginally subsistent small farmers and miners of East Tennessee to fight against the Confederacy and most of their fellow Southerners in the War Between the States. More skeptical historians suggest that envy also had something to do with it: Most of the eastern hill people were too poor to afford slaves themselves and resented more affluent neighbors to the south and west, with their richer soil, and sprawling plantations cultivated by slave labor.

Hence the historic anomaly of the poorest, most backward region of Tennessee being the most Republican, while almost everywhere else in the South (with the exception of a few similar population pockets in nearby border states like Kentucky), the same sort of voters would have been red-neck Democratic populists since time immemorial. East Tennessee is a standing refutation of economic determinism in politics; it proves that family and regional traditions, old feuds and ties of blood and emotion are sometimes stronger than the lure of the welfare state.

At the same time, the comparative poverty of the region and

its relative freedom from the taint of racism makes a man like Howard Baker less of a typical southern politician of the old conservative Bourbon variety. Like their East Tennessean constituents, most of the region's congressmen have tended to be a curious blend of archconservative and progressive. When you chop that mixture up into small enough pieces it comes out "moderate." This helps to explain Howard Baker's own political outlook and voting record. Americans for Constitutional Action, for example, rate Baker at 67 percent, a passing but far from glowing standing in conservative circles, while the liberal Americans for Democratic Action allow him 13 percent—a score, while low, far higher than that of many other southern and conservative Republican legislators. It also helps to explain Baker's ability to attract a surprisingly large chunk of Tennessee's Black vote—30 percent in his last (1978) Senate race.

If his home region is poor, the same cannot be said of Howard Baker. Like Polonius, he practices moderation in all things, including wealth. At 5' 7", Howard Baker is probably the smallest millionaire in the United States Senate, both physically and fiscally. Most of his outside earnings in recent years have come from business investments in Tennessee and speaking fees. When Baker filed the financial statement required by the new federal ethics law in mid-1979 he reported assets of at least $625,000 and, between January 1, 1978 and April 30, 1979, an income of $313,000 in addition to his $57,500 senate salary. Which is about what one would expect of a lawyer turned politician from a fairly well-off old Tennessee family.

The rest of the pattern fits as well. Educated at a private military school in Tennessee, Baker volunteered at 17 for a naval electrical engineering program and later saw service in the Pacific aboard a PT boat. Unlike John Kennedy, he avoided being rammed by any large enemy craft and was discharged unsung but unscathed in 1946 as a junior lieutenant. Then it was law school at the University of Tennessee and a place with his grandfather's law firm in Huntsville where Baker, predictably, excelled as a courtroom debater. In 1964 he made an unsuccessful run in the special Senate election held after the death of Estes Kefauver, learned from his defeat, and in 1966, with the Democrats in disarray after a bitter primary fight, became the first popularly elected Republican senator in the history of Tennessee.

Baker's moderate outlook and background are reflected in his issue positions. As a senator he has:

• Generally favored increased defense spending.
• Backed the White House on Vietnam from LBJ through Jerry Ford.
• Opposed forced school busing to achieve racial balance.
• Favored removal of price controls on domestic oil and gas.
• Generally opposed deficit spending, although the constitutional amendment he favors to require a balanced federal budget would include an escape clause allowing emergency deficit spending under certain circumstances.

At the same time, Baker's more liberal positions have included:

• Support for open housing legislation.
• A stand in favor of medicaid-funded abortions for low income women that could cause trouble in some primaries.
• Backing of windfall profit taxes for American oil companies.
• A characteristically moderate stance on nuclear power, favoring the development of reactor clusters in nuclear "parks" away from population-dense areas.

Like most Republican presidential candidates in 1980, Howard Baker has joined the taxpayers' rebellion, proposing a 30 percent reduction in personal income taxes over three years, combined with reductions in capital-gains and corporate taxes.

More emotionally volatile was Baker's support of the Carter Administration's Panama Canal treaty, which surrendered

American ownership and control of the vital waterway to the Panamanian government—a move that shouldn't hurt Baker much in a general election but that has embittered some Republican conservatives and could be a minor minus in the primaries. Conversely, his opposition to the SALT II arms reduction agreement gains him little if anything, since all of his major GOP opponents have already taken the same stand and his belated joining of the anti-SALT chorus may merely have weakened his standing with the liberal media.

In many ways Baker's cautious, deliberative approach to SALT displays both his strength as a responsible senator and his weakness as a presidential candidate. For months Baker's whole presidential strategy was based on a "senatorial stance" —looking statesmanlike as a leader in the SALT debate. Whether he succeeded in looking statesmanlike or not turns out to be a moot point. The important thing is that hardly anybody was watching, and Baker's heavy investment of time in SALT was, from a political standpoint, a total waste. While Baker was playing the statesman in Washington—probably quite sincerely—his rivals were out in the field organizing.

Like his election to the Senate, Howard Baker's rise to Senate minority leader took more than one attempt. He made unsuccessful bids for the post in 1969 after the death of his father-in-law Everett Dirksen and again in 1971, losing both times to Senator Hugh Scott of Pennsylvania. But in 1977 Baker succeeded in toppling Scott's successor, the sometimes abrasive William Griffin of Michigan. Since then, by all accounts, he has excelled as minority leader and is widely respected by most of his colleagues in both parties. Howard Baker is at home in the Senate—perhaps too much at home. He knows when to conciliate and when to attack, and could well become the most influential Senate leader of either party since Lyndon Johnson if he remains in the chamber—there being a real chance that the GOP will capture a majority for the first time since the 1950s sometime in the next two to four years.

But for the nonce, it is Howard Baker the actual presidential candidate, not Howard Baker the potential Republican Senate majority leader with whom we are concerned. Let's run him through the whims.

BAKER LEADERSHIP (Whim 1)

Shortly before Howard Baker formally announced his presidential candidacy, Senator Barry Goldwater sent him a note: "Dear Howard: You were a leader in Panama and I thought that would kill you. But it didn't." So at least one of the GOP's conservative Senate backbenchers has a grudging respect for Baker's resiliency as a leader. Commenting on the question of his leadership potential as a presidential contender from a different angle, Baker's campaign chairman, Senator Richard Lugar of Indiana, declared that "Howard is uniquely capable of attracting independent and Democratic voters away from Kennedy in key states. . . . That is why both Ted Kennedy and Jimmy Carter have indicated that Howard Baker is the opponent they fear most."

Weighing this argument, the *Washington Star*'s Jules Witcover, one of our more astute political journalists, wrote that

> in political jargon, what Howard Baker has going for him more than any other thing is "electability"—that mysterious alchemy that gives a politician appeal transcending party or ideological lines. It is found both in individuals of overriding charisma, about whom positions on issues don't seem to matter, and in those who can round the sharp edges, seldom offending and projecting themselves as effective conciliators.
>
> The senior senator from Tennessee belongs in the latter category. And at a time when Republican chances of regaining the White House appear to hinge on party unity

and the ability to reach out, there is no doubt it is a valuable characteristic.

David Broder, Witcover's counterpart at the *Washington Post,* took a less optimistic view, acknowledging Baker's legislative abilities but adding that

> Baker's professionalism is of a variety that has not proved popular in presidential nominating contests, even in times when voters were less skeptical of politics than they are today.
>
> Baker is . . . in the tradition of Robert A. Taft, Richard B. Russell, Lyndon B. Johnson, Edmund S. Muskie and Henry M. Jackson—all highly effective senators and all losers in the presidential nomination game, which requires skills different from substantive knowledge and manipulative abilities that are important on the Senate Floor.
>
> Baker is a more personable television performer than any of those men. But he shares with them a certain naivete about, and a certain disdain for, the grubby work of organizing turnouts for caucuses and primaries.

Syndicated columnist and television commentator Joseph Kraft seems to agree. After ticking off the same series of pluses and minuses he adds that the biggest liability to the Baker campaign may be "Baker himself. He behaves much less like a hotshot candidate for the most powerful office in the world than like a Republican senator from the woods of Tennessee —which he happens to be."

So mixed marks to Howard Baker on leadership as applied to the nominating process.

BAKER COMMUNICATION (Whim 2)

In the aftermath of Howard Baker's upset loss to George Bush in last November's Maine straw vote, *Time* magazine concluded that besides proving his organizational superiority, "Bush also demonstrated that he may be a better stump speaker than Baker. Both candidates showed up at a GOP forum in Portland . . . where Bush won . . . much support with a blood-stirring campaign speech." Baker's cool style, while effective on the tube, doesn't usually electrify a live audience. Generally he ad-libs fluent but unexciting truisms in a casual, hands-in-pocket style. As a television star, Baker proved his mettle during the Senate Watergate hearings, but that was something of a special case. Anyone was bound to look smooth, serious and responsible with little ole country lawyer Sam Ervin as his main foil. As a stump campaigner then, Baker, while adequate, definitely ranks behind Reagan, Connally and Bush. His television style, while good, is superior to none of them. His one communication advantage vis-à-vis all three could be in debate. Connally is sharp but strident, Reagan requires more coaching on the issues, and Bush is certainly no better than Baker—especially judged by formal debating standards. But on balance, Howard Baker runs a close but definite fourth as a GOP communicator.

BAKER ORGANIZATION (Whim 3)

A small episode that occurred late in 1979 illustrates Howard Baker's organizational inadequacy. After painstakingly compiling a detailed presentation on a proposed nuts-and-bolts Baker primary strategy, a senior campaign aide finally managed to break through the appointments barrier in Baker's Senate office and get some time blocked off to brief the candidate. He came armed with an impressive array of maps, charts and overlays—probably the first thoroughly professional presentation Baker had access to as a presidential candidate and certainly one which would have given him a vital overview of the real fight for the nomination. About ten minutes into the presentation, the senator yawned, rose from his chair and announced that he had other things to attend to. Baker seems to look on campaign organization as something the menials take care of—like raking the leaves or doing the dishes.

While his campaign organization includes several able, experienced veterans of 1968, 1972 and 1976, there is a chronic lack of commitment at the very top. When things go wrong, as they did in Maine, someone is fired, and his successor finds himself up against the same roadblocks. Thus when campaign chief Don Sundquist, an able Tennessee GOP operative with fifteen years of national party experience, was dropped, Wyatt Stewart, another Republican organizer of similar age and experience, was brought in to replace him—and the campaign and the candidate continued to drift.

Baker's organizational weakness in Iowa, New Hampshire and Florida has led to a fallback scenario of desperation concentrating on the scramble for an early victory somewhere—anywhere—to keep the race alive. The Baker organization is even talking seriously about proving the candidate's "electability" by possible wins in the irrelevant Puerto Rican primary and what political analysts Germond and Witcover have called the "smoke-filled primary" in Arkansas, a rather dubious and hastily-rigged effort which will pit a majority of Reagan backers and Bush forces led by popular Arkansas Representative John Paul Hammerschmidt against a gimcrack Baker organization consisting mainly of creaky remnants of the late Winthrop Rockefeller's gubernatorial machine, now minus the Rockefeller money that keep it oiled in Winthrop's lifetime.

All in all, the Baker organizational story is a sad one. A man of his political stature deserves better, but most of the blame for the current organizational malaise lies at his own door—so much so that some of his more skilled campaign aides have begun murmuring about decamping to Bush or even Reagan unless Baker wakes up and takes command.*

BAKER WAR CHEST (Whim 4)

At the outset of Campaign 1980, Howard Baker had the feeblest war chest of any serious Republican contender. Besides trailing behind Connally, Reagan and Bush in fundraising (in that order) he was also led by lame-duck conservative candidate Philip Crane. At one point early in the race, before he had formally announced, Baker even temporarily lost $16,000 in contributions—not to another candidate but to ABC News! It appears that a package containing $16,000 in checks was mistakenly handed over to an ABC News courier instead of a messenger from ABC Lockbox, Inc., the firm responsible for depositing Baker campaign contributions. Instead of making it to the bank that afternoon, the erstwhile checks ended up on the ABC Evening News. That would seem to say it all about the state of Baker's war chest, but there is a brighter side.

While Howard Baker has lost out on most of the big early money from national Republican contributors, he can still count on strong support from the financial heart of the Mid-South—the Nashville banking community. Support from this source, if Baker is as popular as he claims to be in his native state, should keep him afloat until—and *if*—his campaign begins to move nationally. The moment he shows some real strength in the primaries, Baker's name recognition, his moderate stance and his high standing in the Senate should be an irresistible lure to assorted fat cats and those members of the GOP's moderate northeasten wing who have not already committed themselves to George Bush.

On War Chest, then, Baker is down but not out.

*Several, led by political director Bernie Windom, who repeatedly tried and failed to make Baker wake up to his organizational problems, left in disillusionment last December.

BAKER AGE/HEALTH (Whim 5)

At 54 Howard Baker is the youngest major GOP contender. Despite his love for tennis and an avid enthusiasm for amateur photography that keeps him out of doors during much of his leisure time, his short frame tends to pudginess—especially between diets. He is a nonsmoker and a light drinker, enjoying only an occasional gin and tonic. Some staffers complain of Baker's intermittent lethargy as a campaigner and weariness in dealing with detail work. But his health is sound and in no way a minus. What Baker does lack is an image of dynamism —the kind of radiant vitality that an ideal candidate gives off. So, satisfactory but not outstandingly high marks to Howard Baker on Age/Health.

BAKER MARRIAGE/FAMILY (Whim 6)

In 1951 Baker married Joy Dirksen, the daughter of Senator Everett Dirksen of Illinois. The couple has a married son, Darek, who works in a Murfreesboro, Tennessee bank and a daughter, Cynthia, who is an assistant television producer in Nashville. "Cissy" is a devoted daughter and a vivacious campaigner who should prove an asset in the race. Mrs. Baker could present something of a problem. For years, wild but whispered stories of Joy Baker's behavior while drinking were a standard commodity among Capitol Hill gossips, and more recently Mrs. Baker publicly acknowledged that she is a reformed alcoholic. She has reportedly kept on the wagon for more than three years now. It was Mrs. Baker's drinking problem that many insiders blamed for Gerald Ford's passing over Howard Baker and selecting Kansas Senator Bob Dole as his running mate in 1976—although concern about support in midwestern farm states probably played as great a part in the decision as Joy's tippling. Mrs. Baker also has the reputation, deserved or not, of being something less than the ideal candidate's wife, occasionally berating her diminutive husband in front of large audiences when—as happened at one recent Baker appearance in New England—she takes exception to the seating arrangements or other trifles. She has also been known to confuse scheduling and turn a bit snappish in social gatherings with some of her husband's big contributors. On the evidence, Mrs. Baker would not seem much of a plus as a potential First Lady, but she certainly isn't in-and-of-herself that significant a liability either. And if heredity counts for anything, the daughter of Ev and Louella Dirksen is bound to have reservoirs of untapped charm and intelligence that may yet come into play.

On Marriage/Family, then, Baker comes out with a mixed but basically positive rating.

BAKER WILD CARD (Whim 7)

Howard Baker's entire political career has been based on integrity and a sense of calm moral balance. I have yet to hear anyone—including his most inveterate conservative foes in the Senate and other GOP circles—express anything but personal respect for him as a man. His earned reputation for individual integrity was publicly enhanced by the televised 1974 Senate Watergate hearings in which Baker emerged as the most objective, intelligent man on the committee in the public's perception—so much so that in one poll taken at the time, he led Teddy Kennedy as a potential presidential candidate. Except for the chance of some minor family embarrassment, his scandal factor seems to be nil.

In his thirteen years in the Senate, the nearest thing to a breach of ethics he was ever charged with concerned a half-forgotten land deal involving a tract of Tennessee wilderness with considerable timber, coal and gas resources, part-ownership of which he inherited from his father. In 1966 Baker ran as a foe of strip mining, but as reporter David Ashenfelter subsequently wrote in the *Detroit News,* in 1974 . . . more than half of the tract was reopened to strip mining. Baker, who reportedly hoped to earn $500,-000 in the first three years of a new coal lease, was branded as a hypocrite.

If this is the worst nugget investigative journalism can dig up on Howard Baker's ethical conduct, even allowing for the slight risk of family embarrassments, he comes up with a very safe Wild Card rating.

Having concluded Baker's *Seven Deadly Whims,* let me add a short postscript. In my introduction to this book I stated that I was "not all that impressed with the candidate class of 1980. Some of the most qualified presidential material in both parties is, as of this writing, either out of the running by choice, or very much in the underdog category." Baker is a case in point. My respect for Howard Baker as a senator and my belief that he has the makings of a sound President are equalled only by my doubts about his ability as a candidate for the nomination. He may still wake up to his organizational problems before it is too late. But I really don't believe he has enough of the ugly but all-too-often necessary obsession with the White House that motivates most successful presidential candidates. I suspect that he simply will not run hard or cleverly enough to make up for the ground he has already lost.

I also believe he has a great continued role to play as a leader in the Senate. One more curious wrinkle. Baker, if willing, would make an ideal vice presidential candidate for almost any of the other major GOP contenders. He could probably deliver the South for them, would be a real help in soothing and holding moderate-to-liberal Republicans and attracting independent voters, and would be an asset as a television campaigner. The other side of the question is whether or not there would be anything in it for Howard Baker. That would depend on who the presidential nominee was, and whether or not Baker thinks that the Vice Presidency is worth swapping for a safe Senate seat and a possible future as majority leader.

Many who have occupied the number two slot in the White House have come away disillusioned, agreeing with one of FDR's long string of former Veeps, "Cactus Jack" Garner, that the Vice Presidency—to use Garner's vivid Texas phraseology —"isn't worth a bucketful of warm spit."* Baker would lose nothing by running for the post *if* the Republicans lost in 1980, and he would build up a lot of national I.O.U.s for a possible future presidential try. After the November voting, in the event of a GOP loss, he would simply return to the Senate and serve out the remaining four years of his term with all options open. However, if the GOP ticket with Baker as Veep were to win the White House in 1980, he would have to resign from the Senate and serve four to eight years of vice presidential servitude (unless, as William Buckley once threatened to do if elected mayor of New York, he successfully demanded a recount).

The only circumstances under which the Vice Presidency could be valuable to Baker would be with Ronald Reagan as President. Then, with Reagan pushing seventy-four by the time the 1984 elections rolled around, Baker as his Veep, would be the automatic heir. Worth thinking about, if not betting on.

*Several journalistic old-timers who knew Garner well have told me that the fluid he referred to was something other than spit, but that the more discreet editing policy of the era bowdlerized the quote for family consumption. We may never know, but the watered down version is strong enough.

5. WAITING IN THE WINGS . . .

Never do today what you can do tomorrow. Something may occur to make you regret your premature action.
—Aaron Burr (Vice President, retired)

There are a number of declared Republican candidates for the Presidency who have little if any chance of making it to the finish line. You will find them summarized in Part IV: Odds, Ends, Creeps and Veeps. *But in the 1980 Republican ranks there are two special cases, men who could become serious contenders at the very last minute, but who will sit out the preliminaries of the race. Because of a combination of factors—personal popularity, depth of experience and acceptability as compromise figures—both deserve consideration as men the Republican Party might well turn to in the unlikely eventuality of a deadlocked convention.*

Such a deadlock, while not very probable in 1980, is still possible. Even its remote likelihood gives both former President Gerald Ford and General Alexander Haig at least as much of a crack at the GOP nomination as the officially declared longshots we will discuss in Part IV.

Besides being the two men most likely to offer the Republican Party a noncontroversial way out of a convention stalemate, Ford and Haig share another special trait. Both of them have already been tested in the White House—Haig as a day-to-day surrogate leader with near-presidential powers during the closing weeks of the Wa-

tergate ordeal, and Ford as an actual, if unelected, President serving out the duration of Nixon's second term after the latter's resignation in 1974.

Thus Ford and Haig deserve to be taken seriously as proven presidential material if not as active nomination contenders. In the brief sections that follow, I have tried to give the reader thumbnail evaluations of both men. Having worked closely with Ford and Haig in the White House myself, there isn't much that I've had to guess about—I've seen both of them at ease and in crisis, and I must confess at once that I think the nation—and the Republican Party—could do a lot worse than to chose either of them. Having said that, I should also add that I very much doubt that either Ford or Haig will be nominated.

Stranger things though have happened in American politics, and this book is intended to handicap longshots as well as favorites. However, since neither Ford nor Haig has a full-fledged organization in the field with large-scale staffs, war chests or strategies, they can't be rated using the full Seven Deadly Whims, *but only in concise verbal sketches.*

As General Haig would be the first to admit, rank has its privileges. So I am sure he won't object to our starting with former President Jerry Ford.

Jerry Ford: Beloved Bumbler

*I'll never forget old
what's-his-name.*

—Anonymous

HE STUMBLED. HE mumbled. He bumbled. He had a penchant for bumping into things and falling down stairs. He prematurely liberated Poland and discovered an exotic new disease called "Sickle Cell Armenia." He told us that he was a Ford, not a Lincoln—but some of us suspected him of being an Edsel. Many of us laughed at him, dismissing him as an accidental (and accident-prone) President.

But through it all, Jerry Ford did a fairly adequate job of running the country and restoring confidence in the White House. And in retrospect he doesn't look too bad. Whatever his personal limitations, his twenty-five years of congressional experience had left him familiar with most national issues and the *modus operandi* for getting things done in Washington. Ford was also taken seriously by most foreign leaders and succeeded in maintaining the national self-respect (and a measure of American prestige abroad) in spite of the fall of South Vietnam, Laos and Cambodia. At home, Ford grappled with inflation with better results than his successor and enjoyed a superior working relationship with the legislative branch in spite of overwhelming Democratic majorities in both houses of the Congress. He left the White House personally popular after a hair's breadth defeat by Jimmy Carter, and he is generally credited with having kept most of his promises and leaving the country—and the institution of the Presidency—in better shape than he found them.

If a large chunk of the Democratic Party feels nostalgia for Camelot and the 1960s, a substantial minority of Republicans still feel the same way about Jerry Ford. Looking back to 1976 in a humorous essay in the *Washington Post,* Senator Bob Dole (whose lively sense of humor seldom comes across on camera and is one of the best kept secrets in Washington) indulged in a bit of fond and only slightly tongue-in-cheek nostalgia for the Ford years.

Malaise then was something you felt after partying late, or in confronting the national debt. The Cabinet was not subject to purge at the first sign of individual talent. No one confused Betty Ford with Madame LaFarge.

The only thing President Ford was interested in whipping was inflation. And he was doing a pretty fair job at it, too—the inflation rate for his last full year in office was 4.8 percent, compared with 13.2 percent for the first half of 1979. By contrast, Jimmy Carter may leave the White House with a job approval rating lower than the rate of inflation during his first term in office.

I suspected we might have problems abroad the first time I heard Jimmy Carter refer to his great friends, the Eye-talians. It's been downhill ever since.

Columnist George Will, after a long meeting with the former President at his Vail, Colorado, vacation home, came away in a similar mood. "Ford's place in history is, for the moment, clear," he wrote.

> He is the man the country was fortunate to find at hand when it needed a president it could read as an open, and not very complicated book. You might think he would be glad to saunter on down the road of life without looking back. But the nagging ache of his narrow defeat in 1976 has been only partly assuaged by the knowledge that, today, most Americans probably believe that the country made the wrong choice.

Because of his popularity—and the lingering feeling that Ronald Reagan played a spoiler's role in 1976—Jerry Ford has toyed with the role of titular head of the GOP ever since he left the White House in 1977. He appears frequently as a speaker at party fundraisers where—although a modest orator at best—he is always warmly received. His message is a simple one: "These are tough times. The real world is a dangerous place that needs stable, dependable leadership—leadership that avoids the ideological fringes and seeks to unite our country. That is the challenge of 1980."

But Jerry Ford always draws back from making a real commitment to run. "I do better in the polls when I'm not a candidate, so why become one?" he quips.

He's right. An autumn 1979 poll taken by the *Boston Globe* found that Jerry Ford, the noncandidate without a campaign organization, nosed out Ronald Reagan by 38 percent to 34 percent among New Hampshire Republicans. Such figures count for nothing since Ford won't enter the primary and is waiting—almost certainly in vain—to be drafted. But they add an ironic edge to his paean on the joys of the retired life: "Betty and I have found that retirement is not all that bad . . . and I would recommend it for President Carter at the earliest possible date."

At 66 Jerry Ford still looks and acts like a man in his late forties, but not a man who burns for a return match to the point of actively campaigning for the nomination. And as George Will puts it, "in order for him to be nominated, six or so improbable things have to happen in an improbable sequence." Reagan must falter, John Connally's balloon must burst, the Bakerbush must wither, and a long string of dark horses actively in the race must go lame. Worst of all, the GOP would have to virtually declare itself bankrupt of new faces. Selecting Ford in 1980 would be a public confession that the best his party had to offer was a fairly old, only moderately effective campaigner who was rejected by the voters in 1976.

Not bloody likely. Still, because he does hold a seemingly permanent place in the public's esteem—and because many people who voted for Jimmy Carter in 1976 seem to have concluded that it was a big mistake—one shouldn't dismiss Ford as a long shot.

Because he is not an officially declared candidate, we can't give him a complete rating on the *Seven Deadly Whims,* but we can summarize his assets and liabilities.

Leadership: Proven performance, lackluster but sound as a sitting President. A warm, fatherly presence radiating sturdy reliability. Few real enemies in the party or among the electorate—but few really avid backers, too.

Communication: Less talented as a stump speaker than all of the major declared GOP contenders but capable of good low-key interviews and adequate as a television presence in professionally produced film spots. A plausible figure with experience.

Organization: Nonexistent beyond a small personal staff that handles his correspondence, speaking schedule and routine activities as a retired President. Most of the professional talent involved in his '76 campaign, from chairman Jim Baker (now heading the Bush effort) on down, are already actively backing other candidates. Some of the tired hacks who did such a poor job of writing, planning and counseling—mainly old staff cronies from the Congress who were a constant embarrassment in the Ford White House and who sabotaged much of the good work done by solid pros like Don Rumsfeld and Dick Cheney in '76—would be glad to hitch up with a new Ford candidacy. But their kind of help Jerry Ford doesn't need. If nominated, on the other hand, Ford could draw on the best talent from every spectrum of the GOP—but his non-candidacy will probably not progress that far.

War Chest: Again, virtually nonexistent. A late declaration would bring in some money, especially if it were to coincide with Reagan slippage. But in an already crowded field, most of the big money has long since chosen its favorites from among the running entries. Again, *if* nominated, Ford would probably be able to quickly generate all the money he needed from both wings of the GOP. But it just isn't likely to come to that.

Age/Health: Jerry Ford is no spring chicken, but he has kept well and has plenty of stamina. He looks healthy and active and he is. No problem here.

Marriage/Family: Betty Ford is still one of the most admired women in America. Her victory over alcoholism and overmedication was more inspiring than scandalous, and her openness in discussing it seems to have made her far more friends than enemies. The Ford kids, while prone to running at the mouth occasionally, look good, are better behaved than the Carters, and, on the whole, would be a campaign plus. All's well on the family front.

Wild Card: When it comes to wild cards, Jerry Ford is not dealing with a full deck. We probably know more about him—the kind of man he is and the kind of politician and leader he is—than we do about anyone else in the field, including Jimmy Carter. The single blot on his record that a substantial minority of Americans seem to have held against him in 1976 was his blanket pardon of Richard Nixon. This may still cost him some support. But most people have worse things to be enraged about nowadays. So a wild card plus because of the *lack* of potential Ford surprises.

In summary then, Ford is another of the men I would categorize as good presidential material with only the slimmest of chances to win the nomination. As a member of his White House staff for more than a year, and as a consultant in his '76 campaign operation, I came to feel a mild personal affection and a certain respect for the man. In many ways I believe that he is the sort of leader America and the democratic West need today even more than they did when he was in the White House.

He really *is* what he seems—a strong, thoughtful man of experience who reasons and acts clearly even though he occasionally stumbles physically and verbally. But Ford's time as a nominee—as opposed to his usefulness as an elected leader—has probably come and gone. As one prominent Republican fundraiser put it in a recent private chat, "If Jerry couldn't hack it as an incumbent President with the White House and most of the party leadership behind him in '76, how can you expect him to get off the ground in '80 as an old-age pensioner with no organization to speak of?"

Personally, while it may be the country's loss, I suspect it's Jerry Ford's gain. He's already made a substantial contribution to American history. He's won a real if limited place in the affection of his countrymen and will be able to play the role of popular elder statesman as much or as little as he wants to for the rest of his life. Why jeopardize it, especially since it could mean an anticlimactic and humiliating defeat at the end of a long, positive career?

I'm reminded of a conversation I had in January of 1977 with another federal retiree. After an hour of reminiscing about the 1940s and 1950s (I had just finished some editing work for the gentleman in question on the portion of his memoirs covering that period), my companion abruptly switched the subject to the present. "What do people think about Jerry Ford?" he asked, obviously really wanting to know how Ford measured up in public esteem compared to his immediate predecessor.

It was a moment that called for equal parts of candor and discretion. I paused for a second, gazing out the window at the shimmering San Clemente coastline as a rather mangy Irish setter passed by, enjoying his afternoon walk with Manolo, my host's Portuguese valet.

"Ford's left office with a clean slate (ouch!) and a residue of genuine affection," I replied. "But I think most voters have closed the file on him. He'll stay popular as long as he stays retired."

My host rubbed his blue-gray chin thoughtfully and nodded. "Yeah," said Richard Nixon.

May they both rest in peace, say I.

Alexander Haig: Ike Redivivus?

The last thing the GOP needs
in 1980 is a man on dark-horseback.
                                   —Ben Buncombe

        I BEGIN THIS short essay on Alexander Haig from a rather unenviable vantage point. How do you gracefully write off someone you like, respect and believe would be a good President? Worse yet, as I stare over my typewriter at the north wall of my study, a photograph of Alexander Haig smiles back at me, the steely blue eyes blissfully unaware of what I am about to write, and the inscription "To Aram Bakshian with gratitude, friendship and admiration for your service to country and president" a bit embarassing under the circumstances. That's politics for you.

First the good news. Alexander Haig, at 54, is probably the most politically experienced nonpolitician in the race. For weeks he practically ran the White House and much of the Federal government while the Nixon Presidency foundered. I was there at the time, and I know that he was good at it. Haig has also proven himself as a combat leader, a soldier-statesman as the most respected NATO commander since Eisenhower, and a foreign policy expert whose skill at personal diplomacy was such that he survived for years as the senior assistant to the prickly and demanding Henry Kissinger.

He is intelligent, well-read, a firm leader with a low-key, deceptively easy manner, and an excellent organizer and administrator. He understands power and is learning about electioneering fast. He is a Catholic, which would lend some strength to a national Republican ticket but is not likely to matter one way or the other in the race for the nomination. He is also a dapper dresser (within the bounds of Ivy League good taste) and uses a long "a"—both minor but far from frivolous aids in winning support from the East Coast moderate wing of the GOP.

In fact one's impression of Al Haig is not so much that of a retired soldier as of a smart, assured banker or diplomat—a product of Princeton or Yale rather than West Point. He speaks with a calm authority, in the manner of a man whose orders issue from the executive suite rather than the battlefield. He is sleek but not slick. A proper Philadelphian who comes across as sincere, purposeful.

Now for the bad news. Haig has all of the qualities of a successful nominee except for the indispensable one—a solid base of electoral and organizational support. He has been slow to enter the race and many who might have rallied to his banner earlier are already ensconced with Reagan, Baker, Connally or Bush. It is unlikely that anything happening between now and the Detroit convention will dislodge enough of them—or galvanize enough rank-and-file GOP voters—to win Al Haig the nomination. In his most candid moments, he seems to know it. "I think I am as promising a national candidate as there is in the field," Haig told *Washington Post* reporter Kathy Sawyer in November of 1979, "and the least nominatable."

Again one is faced with the grand paradox of presidential politics—the contradictory pulls of nomination appeal and general electoral appeal. The best that Haig's organizers can hope for in the primaries is table scraps—strong voter turnout among retired military personnel in Florida, where there are quite a few of them; favorite son sentiment in Haig's native Pennsylvania; and a smattering of moderate and mildly conservative votes from Republicans looking for a "nonpolitical" alternative a la Eisenhower.

By clinging to these rather slender political reeds, and hoping Reagan stumbles without any one of his major challengers being able to supplant him, Haig just might end up the choice of a deadlocked convention. It's an updated, more activist variation of the Ford waiting game scenario—a semicandidacy rather than a noncandidacy to draw a somewhat precious distinction. Hence, as with Ford, we can only give Alexander Haig an abbreviated *Seven Deadly Whims* evaluation.

> *Leadership:* Strong potential perception as a leader qualified to handle foreign crises and restore American prestige and military power. Clean-cut "good soldier" image, but without the war hero status of Eisenhower. On the debit side are the lack of any elective experience and the lingering aroma of the Nixon White House.
>
> *Communication:* Haig is very effective as an interviewee and screen presence; a little tepid and rambling as a stump speaker. He has good potential as a debater working within a structured, rational format. Haig looks and sounds presidential in a more subdued, up-to-date way than Connally—the affable, manly executive look rather than that of the flamboyant, silver-maned, slightly overpowering politico. Fine communication potential, then, but *only* potential unless it can be funded, packaged and transmitted to an awful lot of GOP voters in a very short time.
>
> *Organization:* Haig's organizational spadework was done for him in the autumn of 1979 by two experienced GOP

operatives, Charlie MacManus and Lew Helm. The small draft committee they set up has since been expanded, and Haig has also received valuable organizational input from Stuart Spencer, Jerry Ford's chief political advisor in 1976, and South Carolinian Harry Dent, one of the creator's of Richard Nixon's successful Southern Strategy. This all adds up to an adequate force for a holding action—but nothing near the scale of operation needed to win the nomination in the field as opposed to at a brokered convention.

War Chest: Again, adequate for a holding operation and with potential for much more. Haig himself has already proven a very popular speaker at fundraisers—in the first eighteen weeks after he resigned as NATO commander, he addressed influential audiences in thirty-four states and was generally well received. The money—and the willingness to contribute it—is out there. But Haig has to show potential supporters something tangible in the way of primary votes before anything approaching a band-wagon mentality forms and the financial trickle becomes a flood.

Age/Health: At 54 Al Haig is vigorously healthy and at the peak of his mental powers. He has a strongly positive physical presence. No problem here.

Marriage/Family: For a public personality, Haig's private life has been surprisingly neglected by the media. The reason is two-fold—no skeletons in the closet and a wife and children who have never had to campaign or court publicity. So no negative *Marriage/Family* factor and a mild plus for bland inoffensiveness.

Wild Card: The word is Watergate. How much does Haig's presence as White House chief of staff in the last days of the Nixon Administration handicap him as a candidate? On the negative side, reporter Donald Kimelman summed up the problem concisely in the *Philadelphia Inquirer:* "The Watergate tapes . . . show that Haig, like so many others around Nixon, helped to devise ways of keeping the full truth . . . from emerging. . . . He was among those who advised Nixon in the so-called Saturday

Night Massacre, which resulted in the resignation of Attorney General Elliott Richardson and the firings of Watergate special prosecutor Archibald Cox and Deputy Attorney General William Ruckelshaus. The tapes show that Haig also suggested to Nixon that he could say that he didn't remember when confronted with potentially damaging questions."

On the other hand, as Haig himself has said, "In the aggregate, I'm not the least bit self-conscious about that experience. . . . You know there have been at least a score of books written . . . by advocates and opponents, from Judge Sirica to Leon Jaworski . . . and I don't know of one that had any concerns or questions about my performance during that period. I was scrutinized by three grand juries, a court of law and two Senate investigating committees, and in no instance was there a derogatory question or remark made about my performance." On balance, I would suspect that Haig's *Wild Card* minus on Watergate is countered by the plus factor chance of more Americans turning to a nonpolitical technocrat with military and foreign policy experience if—as is quite possible—events in Iran and elsewhere around the world grow even more explosive.

Where does all of this leave Alexander Haig? Perhaps in the White House, but probably as Vice President at best. As a Catholic and a Pennsylvanian, he would be an excellent complement to any Republican head of ticket from the South, the Southwest or the Midwest. He would also lend important credibility to any candidate weak on foreign policy and national-security experience. And in the case of Reagan, he would be a strong back-up man whose age and vitality were adequate without posing too much of an embarrassingly youthful, pink-cheeked contrast to the aging Californian.

Haig would also be a good candidate for the Pennsylvania Senate seat being vacated by Richard Schweiker, despite his repeated insistence that he is "not a committeeman" and isn't interested in the Senate. But, granted the unlikelihood of a Haig presidential nomination, I see his major future contribution in the specialties he knows best. In any Republican Administration, Al Haig would make an ideal Secretary of Defense or Secretary of State. At a time when our military strength has slipped dangerously and our allies have lost much faith in our strength and resolve, the skill and prestige Haig would bring to either post would do the country a great deal of good. Here's hoping.

As I pointed out in my introduction, every presidential race is a sort of civic scavenger hunt. One has to sift through a lot of dross in order to get to the valuables. In the last two sections of this book, we have scrutinized the potential winners in the 1980 sweepstakes. Here we will take a more fleeting glimpse at the near-certain losers, has-beens, never-weres and one or two Quixotic characters who probably deserve better but don't stand a chance. Having done that, we will then take a quick speculative look at some of the possible vice-presidential permutations and, in Part V, put together our final handicapping.

Charles Dickens, perhaps the greatest verbal caricaturist ever to work in the English language, once observed that there are only two kinds of portraiture, the serious and the smirking. We have now reached the smirking stage. What follows, depending on one's mood, is a brisk evaluation of doomed also-rans in the order of their descending gravity or increasing absurdity. Let's begin with a border-line case—a man who is either the most serious of the frivolous candidates or the most frivolous of the serious candidates, Senator Bob Dole of Kansas.

PART IV

Odds, Ends, Creeps & Veeps

*Many shall run to and fro, and knowl-
edge shall be increased.*
—Ezekiel 12:14

Your public servants serve you right.
—Adlai Stevenson

Bob Dole

Nature has given Bob Dole the swarthy good looks of a "B" film villain. If he had been born in Transylvania instead of Kansas, he would probably be cashing in on the current Dracula revival rather than running for President. Even his excellent sense of humor fits the part. It is bitingly mordant. Yet Dole is a true *homme serieuse* in the Senate and at least as intelligent and experienced as most of his more successful rivals for the nomination. He is also refreshingly outspoken— much too much so for his own good as a national candidate.

Columnist James Kilpatrick recently went so far as to suggest that, if Diogenes were still alive, he would willingly snuff his lantern after a meeting with the senior Senator from Kansas, his age-old search for an honest man finally "crowned with success. Bob Dole is his kind of guy." But even Kilpatrick felt constrained to add that Dole's race for the nomination is pretty hopeless. "In most of his polls," writes Kilpo, "he ranks two points behind None of the Above."

Except for the image problem already cited, it's hard to understand why Bob Dole is not taken very seriously by his party as a presidential candidate. He is probably the most able spokesman for the rural Midwest in the United States Senate—a leading champion of the traditional Republican heartland. He occupied important posts in local government before being elected to the House of Representatives in 1960 and winning two tough, uphill battles for the Senate in 1968 and 1974. He was a much decorated platoon leader in World War II, who was literally blown to pieces in action. Dole's incredible rehabilitation after thirty-nine months of hospitalization and multiple surgery is positive proof of the man's moral and physical strength, and a possible clue to his rather acid attack on "Democratic wars" during his 1976 vice-presidential debate with Fritz Mondale who, like his political mentor Hubert Humphrey, never wore his country's uniform. Dole has paid his dues as a soldier, a citizen, and a legislator.

He also earned an impressive list of Republican IOUs as the GOP's national committee chairman from 1971 to 1973, a post to which he brought his customary energy and conscientiousness. In 1976, as Jerry Ford's running mate, Dole helped carry much of rural America for the ticket. But he also seems to have frightened off an indeterminate number of moderate voters and has been cast by many commentators—wrongly in my opinion—as a decisive negative factor in what was a painfully close race.

The acerbic side of Bob Dole's personality has also earned him the reputation of being a difficult man to work with. The rapid turnover of his Capitol Hill staff is legendary, ranking up there with such all-time staff cannibals as former Representative Bella Abzug. His campaign staff has been plagued by the same problem. Dole drives himself hard and does the same to his employees—but their capacity for hard work (and ability to absorb his verbal barbs when something goes wrong) is seldom up to the job.

I got to know Bob Dole fairly well in 1971 when I was one of the first people he brought onto the Republican National Committee's communications operation upon assuming the chairmanship. I liked him but found him a moody fellow to work for—uncommunicative from a speechwriter's point of view and always torn between his desire to speak the unspeakable and toe the safe middle line. It was an interesting year and I left for the White House with a high estimate of Dole's ethics and intelligence, but with serious doubts about his ability to assemble and hold a top notch team—and then get good mileage out of it. This would probably be his most serious weakness as a President and nominee, but it is also the main reason he is unlikely to become either.

One hopes he will decide to run for reelection to the Senate, where he plays the useful role of gadfly, serving as an accomplished advocate for rural America and a moderately conservative GOP wheelhorse of proven stamina. Bob Dole's ironic humor would be missed, as witness the following explanation for why he didn't take his 1976 vice-presidential defeat to heart:

> I may have selfish reasons for so graciously accepting our loss in 1976. As senior Senator from Kansas, ranking Republican on the Senate Finance Committee and a former GOP national chairman, I'm occasionally noticed in Washington restaurants. I have no trouble hailing a cab. Had Jerry Ford won, all that would have changed. I would have been Vice President.

I suspect that the same benign providence that spared Bob Dole that thankless job will deliver the rest of us from a Dole Presidency in 1981. Until then, clutch tightly to your wolfbane; keep those garlic cloves handy.

Phil Crane

If Bob Dole could have made a comfortable living in vampire films of the tonier sort, 49-year-old Representative Phil Crane of Illinois seems designed by fate to play the male romantic lead in any future remake of *Tammy and the Bachelor*. His handsome, clean-cut appearance and militant conservatism have made him the matinee idol of the right-wing banquet circuit. Crane is especially titillating to Republican matrons of a certain age—the Shaun Cassidy of the GOP Geritol set.

More impressive are his educational credentials. Having completed his undergraduate studies at DePauw University, Hillsdale College, the University of Michigan and the University of Vienna, Phil Crane earned his master's and doctorate in history at Indiana University. He is one of the few trained historians in the Congress, and there must be moments when he wonders what he is doing there.

Crane first ran for the House of Representatives in a 1969 special election. He has been overwhelmingly reelected by his affluent suburban Chicago constituents ever since. His efforts to build a broader national following have yielded more mixed results. In 1977 he was elected chairman of the American Conservative Union, the leading "respectable" right-wing national action committee. Crane gave up the post in early 1979 when his active candidacy for the presidential nomination aroused protests from pro-Reagan elements in the A.C.U., but much of his rather thin national support can still be traced to the contacts he made as A.C.U. chairman—a post that gave him national credentials as a conservative spokesman.

Crane has also written several books, most recently *Surrender in Panama,* a lively short polemic on the canal controversy, which appeared in 1978 while Crane was leading a national campaign against the Carter treaty. Though I say it who shouldn't, it is not a bad little book, full of historical nuggets and an almost racy style. At any rate that's how it reads to me, and I have had ample time to study it since I happened to be the principal draftsman on the project. As a literary client, I have to give Phil Crane excellent marks—aside from adding one or two footnotes and eliminating a few obscure historical items, he signed off on the manuscript with a minimum of fuss. The whole thing was the work of a few weeks and ended up, I am told, selling several hundred thousand copies. I once even encountered a Brooklyn cab driver who had read it and approved—high praise indeed.

Not all those who have had professional dealings with Phil Crane leave with such a warm glow, however. Most of the progress he made in his early-bird presidential campaign was erased when he lost the services of direct-mail fundraiser Richard Viguerie and, reportedly at the bidding of his rather volatile wife, Arlene, purged most of his senior campaign aides.

From a theatrical point of view, Arlene Crane has been the most flamboyant character in her husband's campaign. *Washington Post* astrologer "Svetlana" gazed into her crystal ball in August of 1979 and saw what many less arcane observers had already noticed by direct observation. Dismissing Phil Crane as a "very nice man, with a great deal of charm and vivacity," but under the thumb of a domineering and erratic wife, the seeress described Arlene as "born on September 23 but . . . not a Virgo; she is a virago." God, is she ever. Poor Phil Crane— in recent months, when not struggling to pay off his massive campaign debt, he has been plagued by a succession of embarrassing news stories about, interviews of, and public scrapes involving, his little woman.

It all started out, unfairly enough, with a series of hatchet jobs in William Loeb's muckraking Manchester, New Hampshire, *Union Leader,* accusing Arlene, and to a lesser extent her husband, of everything from possible alcoholism to rumored bizarre sex activities. No sooner had these vicious reports been laid to rest, than Arlene went public herself, granting interviews in which she described herself as smarter, prettier and much more eligible for the post of First Lady than Jackie O, Rosalynn, Betty, Pat and Ladybird. She also presided over the purge of the Crane campaign staff, publicly characterizing the people who had been her husband's most trusted aides and the architects of his presidential strategy as the "Rat Patrol" and the "Devil's Triangle." It was clear to all that Phil Crane had been very careless in either his choice of staff or his choice of mate.

Ah, but more was in store. By some quirk of fate, the animal kingdom seems to bear the Crane clan a grudge. On August 25, 1979, at about 4:30 P.M., 18-year-old Susanna M. Crane (one of Phil and Arlene's eight children) was observed "harassing two loons" on Squam Lake. It doesn't pay to fool with Mother Nature, at least not around Squam Lake, New Hampshire,

when your father's running for President. A concerned loono-
phile notified the local authorities, and a written warning was
filed and issued by the New Hampshire Fish and Game Department. Let Scott Sutcliffe, executive director of the New
Hampshire Loon Preservation Committee, have the last word
on this curious little episode.

Interviewed by a local reporter, Sutcliffe stressed that "loons
are a very delicate, easily disturbed species of bird whose habi-
tat is easily destroyed and upset," and that the two loons Ms.
Crane had buzzed in her small green outboard motorboat,
"had very recently given birth to several offspring who are
very vulnerable." Offspring can be such a nuisance at times.

In New Hampshire at least, despite his archconservatism,
Phil Crane had lost the support of the loonatic fringe.

Worse animal acts were to follow. It seems that one of the
four-legged residents of the Crane's suburban Washington
household is a husky black Labrador by the name of Sam. An
avid sportsman, Sam got a little carried away during a game of
catch with the six-year-old son of a Crane neighbor and nipped
him on the wrist.

The incident was reported to the local dogcatcher and,
when Mrs. Crane could produce no evidence that Sam had
been vaccinated for rabies, the authorities routinely attempted to impound him for quarantine. Sam put up no resis-
tance, but Arlene Crane did. She refused to hand him over
and, after a confused exchange of warnings and ill wishes on
both sides, the dogcatcher called in police reinforcements. The
ill-starred Arlene was taken to court and then, after exchang-
ing words with the local magistrate, was ordered to the slam-
mer. At this point she seems to have had second thoughts
about standing up for her rights—or rather sitting down for
them (Mrs. Crane had sat on her hands when an attempt was
made to handcuff her). She reluctantly complied with the magistrate's orders and signed several documents, after which she
was released.

Arlene Crane returned home with understandably frayed nerves and, according to her husband, the presidential candidate, it took "five hours to calm her down." I can believe it.

These assorted grotesque escapades give an idea of the long series of individually unimportant but collectively devastating incidents that have plagued the Crane candidacy and—probably unfairly—rendered an intelligent, thoughtful ideologue absurd in the eyes of many voters. The Crane campaign at the beginning of 1980 was still limping along—mainly in hopes of winning matching federal funding to help pay off its mountainous debts. Richard Viguerie and Crane had managed to raise over $3 million in campaign funds before the end of 1979. But what Viguerie's right hand bestows, his left hand often reclaims. Most of the $3 million was ploughed back into Viguerie's various consulting and direct-mail organizations in the form of expenses and service fees, leaving Crane's campaign $800,000 in the red. Not exactly fiscal conservatism in action.

It's all rather sad—the shabby end to what was once an attractive longshot candidacy. But through it all, Phil Crane seems to have kept his sense of fun and maintained popularity in his home congressional district. He'll probably be around Washington as an articulate, engaging conservative congressman for many years to come; he might even make it into the Senate one of these days—God and Arlene willing. In the meantime, I suspect Phil Crane sometimes finds himself murmuring a sentiment of Beadle Bumble, that henpecked heavy in *Oliver Twist* who, when informed that the law held him responsible for his wife's actions, replied, "If the law supposes that . . . the law is a ass, a idiot."

John Anderson

Pity John Anderson. The pathetic remains of his presidential candidacy will soon lie before us, proof that nothing is more potentially dangerous to a Republican candidate than favorable press coverage from the wrong people. Liberal journalists and broadcasters love John Anderson. They say the nicest things about him. And every time they do they drive another nail into the coffin of his prospects as a GOP contender. "Handsome, bright, articulate, known around town as honest and outspoken," says the *Washington Post* of Anderson, and the candidate himself concedes that he "has wonderful clips," such as the *Des Moines Register*'s glowing description of him as "a silver-haired orator with a golden tongue, a 17-jewel mind and a brass backbone."

But if John Anderson impresses many journalists and some of his Democratic colleagues as a spare-part spellbinder, his standing among Republicans is less formidable. In 1978 he barely survived a conservative primary challenge in his Illinois congressional district. Rumor has it that, rather than risk a humiliating upset there in 1980, he decided to voluntarily retire from the House while there was still time and win a little national publicity (and perhaps a higher asking price as a future partner in a prominent Washington law or lobbying firm) by making a token run for the GOP nomination.

So far, except for garnering tributes from non-Republicans and journalists, he hasn't made a dent. Not that John Anderson hasn't tried. In a vain effort to win massive support from New Hampshire's feminist voters (hardly a big bloc in the Republican primary) he has pulled out all the rhetorical stops, bravely declaring,

> I'm trying to convince women that I'm the best candidate on women's rights. . . . Who else has gone to New Hampshire to participate in a vigil for freedom of choice [on abortion]? I'm putting my body on the line for women.

To which one crusty New Hampshire Republican later countered, "So John Anderson's for abortion, is he? Too bad his parents didn't feel the same way."

Anderson has been called "the best orator in the House of Representatives," usually by people who have only had to listen to him in small doses. While he has a breadth of language and knowledge of history and the law that one would expect from a Phi Beta Kappa and a Harvard man, his speaking style strikes many as pompously preachy—rather like the forensic fireworks of a better-than-average small-town, high school civics instructor who's taken a Dale Carnegie course and read too many of the wrong books about Abraham Lincoln. After a while the rolling sonorities become numbing, almost restful, as you will observe by the nodding heads in the House press gallery whenever John Anderson really gets going. It's like listening to the tide roll in on a drowsy summer day.

Anderson may or may not be right on the issues, but he is running in the wrong party contest. He opposes increased defense spending and supports ratification of SALT II. He denounces what he calls the Pentagon's "missile madness." And he courts women's lib and black votes, which might help in a general election but can only hurt him in the race for the GOP nomination. As 1980 began, he had somehow managed to raise something under $500,000 in campaign funds—more than Larry Pressler and less than Bob Dole.

"I make a lot of speeches that don't make news," complains the man who once thought of becoming a preacher and who, like Jimmy Carter, still enjoys lay sermonizing and an occasional bout of Sunday school lecturing. It could be worse. If more of Anderson's speeches made it into print, his estrangement from the majority of rank-and-file Republicans would be even more complete, and his congressional career might have aborted—no pun intended—years ago.

Anderson's tendency to scold his fellow Republicans as if they were a bunch of benighted heathens and he were a militant fundamentalist missionary, and their tendency in turn to dismiss everything that trills forth from his overworked tonsils as intrinsic hogwash, are both unfortunate. The GOP could learn from John Anderson. And John Anderson, if he ever stopped preaching long enough to listen, might even learn a little from the other members of his party. Despite his proabortion stand, his early opposition to the Vietnam War and his flabby record on defense, he remains more Republican than not—a believer in fiscal responsibility and government encouragement of the private sector and an outspoken advocate of nuclear-generated power.

But it's too late for that now. Lonesome John will soon be one more retired legislator, aware like most of them that you can't go home again, and resigned to spending his comfortable twilight years as a well-paid Washington lawyer or lobbyist. After the first year or so, the dinner and speaking invitations will thin out, and even the *Washington Post* will forget about him. But there'll still be the Sunday school pulpit, the congressional pension and a small circle of admirers willing to listen and listen and listen to his Wilsonian exhortations. The only thing John Anderson really has to fear after the dust settles on the Candidates 1980 is lockjaw. As long as he can keep on talking, "St. John the Righteous," as House Majority Leader Jim Wright has dubbed him, will be happy. And as long as I'm able to stay out of earshot, that's fine with me.

Benjamin Fernandez

Scrappy little Ben Fernandez is a self-made man—but not, as was once said of a cruder *arriviste,* a splendid example of unskilled labor. He was born in a boxcar, of poor Mexican-American parents. As a youth he worked side by side with his seven brothers and sisters in Michigan sugar beet and tomato fields. His parents, he says, "were too proud to seek federal relief." Fernandez agreed—and managed to go remarkably far without it. Working his way through college as a dishwasher and waiter, he earned a degree in economics and started his business career with General Electric in 1951. He earned his

MBA from New York University on the job with G.E., and after a stint as director of marketing research for the O. A. Sutton Corporation, he founded his own prosperous management consulting firm in California in 1960.

Having carved out a successful business career, Fernandez became active in Republican politics, serving as national chairman of the GOP's Hispanic Assembly and as a member of the executive committee of the Republican National Committee. If anyone in the 1980 presidential sweepstakes is a living embodiment of what used to be called the American Dream, it's Ben Fernandez. His rock-ribbed conservatism reflects his sincere if old-fashioned belief in the work ethic and the private sector. Agree with him or not, you've got to respect the man. He doesn't just preach his ethos—he's lived it.

Granted all that, however, one reluctantly concludes that this particularly plucky Don Quixote is doomed to disappointment in the quest for his one really impossible dream, the White House. On paper Ben Fernandez has many of the qualifications of a sound first executive: a good brain, plenty of decision-making and administrative experience and a rude natural eloquence that stems from his deep belief in the old simplicities he espouses.

But the only primary where Fernandez stands a chance of finishing well (and perhaps even winning) is the first and least representative in the race—Puerto Rico. In the February 17th voting in the Commonwealth, Fernandez will probably be the most familiar candidate—certainly the only major Hispanic. And he has focused a large part of his campaigning time and resources on the island. "I think," he says, "Puerto Rico is Fernandez country."

Maybe it is, but chances are that Fernandez country, if it exists at all, probably begins and ends there. A pity really. If Ben Fernandez were a little more liberal, or if he had appeared on the political scene earlier, he just might have been able to pull a Wendell Wilkie in 1980, or at least had a serious crack at the vice-presidential slot. As a Hispanic Catholic he could actually help balance a ticket headed by a WASP like Bush or Baker. I don't see that happening in 1980 and so, on the premise that, as Miguel Cervantes, the creator of the original *Caballero de la Tristo Figura,* put it, " 'tis ill talking of halters in the house of a man that was hanged," I close this brief look at one of the GOP's more appealing might-have-beens.

Larry Pressler

At 37 Larry Pressler has served two terms in the U.S. House of Representatives, and in 1978 won a landslide 68 percent victory in his race for the Senate in South Dakota. A former Rhodes scholar, Army lieutenant in Vietnam and State Department lawyer, bachelor Pressler is one of the more dapper figures on the Senate side, besides being one of the youngest. He seems to find the Senate a dull place, already declaring that he has no intention of spending the rest of his life there. And after a mere eight months in the sedate old chamber, he announced his candidacy for President, calling himself a "moderate conservative" and promising to set forth a platform that will emphasize "promoting gasohol and giving a better break to small business and farms."

But you can't get to the White House on gasohol alone, and reaction, even in Pressler's home state, was less than overwhelming. South Dakota Republican state chairman Dan Parrish had perhaps the pithiest statement: "My reaction in three words would be ha, ha, ha." Said the state's more equivocal Republican governor, Bill Jaklow, "He hasn't got a chance. The election of a President is a very serious thing in America, not to be taken lightly. He has no chance at all of being elected. He knows it, you know it, I know it. He isn't going anyplace . . . I wish him well."

In most of Pressler's postannouncement news photos he is

either grinning or guffawing. Who can blame him? And with a campaign war chest of only $30,000, toothpaste is one of the few things Larry Pressler won't be running short of in 1980. One is put off by the fellow's gall but has to give him a little credit for the sheer dimension of his *geste,* whether it's very *beau* or not.

Harold Stassen

A little respect for the deceased, gentlemen, please . . .

Veeps

And now in the words of the poet Python, for something completely different. Let us try to decipher a few vice-presidential runes before plunging into our final handicapping of the presidential sweepstakes. On the Democratic side, Jimmy Carter must keep Mondale as long as Mondale is interested in saving their marriage for the sake of the Democratic family.

Teddy Kennedy's options are still open, but not all that open. If he wins the nomination he will almost inevitably do what his brother Jack did before him—look South for a running mate. To draw an even tighter parallel, he may well turn to LBJ's Texas and select Senator Lloyd Bentsen, a popular, low-key conservative who would be a great help in cutting Teddy's losses among white Protestants, southern conservatives and nervous members of the private sector across the country. Don't be surprised if it happens.

Another possibility with a different sort of ironic twist is Senator Sam Nunn of Georgia. Besides coming from Carter country, Nunn has a strong record on national defense, is a vigorous, intelligent campaigner, and would serve nearly as well as Bentsen in staunching Democratic bleeding in the constituencies mentioned above. His presence on the ticket would also make it harder for a lame-duck Jimmy Carter to indulge in any anti-Kennedy mischief from the Oval Office. Watch these two men.

Whom Jerry Brown might pick as a running mate in the highly unlikely eventuality of his winning the nomination is something that only his Zen master knows for sure. Good Lord, when you come to think of it, it could easily *be* his Zen master!

The Republican veep possibilities are more extensive if less bizarre. Let us start with the assumption that Reagan heads the ticket. The conventional wisdom early in the campaign was that the best thing Rusty Ronald could do was to recruit a super-young running mate to offset the age issue. Congressman Jack Kemp of New York—a former football star and a bright young conservative from the Northeast—has been the name mentioned most often.

It may well be Kemp, but I would suggest, from the standpoint of Reagan's own best interests, that would be a mistake. Jack Kemp is too *much* younger. His presence on the ticket would tend to aggravate rather than palliate Reagan's age problem much as the sight of a spavined old dowager dancing with a youthful gigolo merely highlights the lady's wrinkles. And Kemp, while he has a good, solid record in Congress and has launched some interesting economic initiatives, is not that much more experienced than Reagan when it comes to foreign affairs, national defense and other weighty issues.

If he could get one of them, it seems to me that Reagan would be far better advised to land Al Haig, Howard Baker or George Bush—all in their fifties, in good shape, without being young enough to pass for Reagan grandchildren. Any one of them would also bring real heft to the Reagan ticket on substantive issues and lend a general image of competency. Let me toss in two other much less talked about names as possible Reagan veeps: Former Treasury Secretary William Simon and Senator William Cohen of Maine. Feisty Bill Simon is a New Jersey Catholic with a loyal national following in business, financial and civic circles. His outspokenness would also make him a joy to follow on the campaign trail. Bill Cohen of Maine is a real longshot, but he may prove to be just the sort of gamble John Sears—Reagan's Cardinal Richelieu—enjoys taking. A popular, attractive New England moderate, Cohen is also of Jewish descent. He would bring a different set of strengths to the ticket and play well in the so far unresponsive Northeast that John Sears seems to woo all the more ardently because of its aloofness. Odd but interesting possibilities there. For the other possible Republican presidential nominess, the veep picture is really too murky for me to make out.

Finally, to revert for a moment to Jimmy Carter, if he should somehow lose Mondale but win the nomination, my instinct says that he would be best advised to choose one of two New York Irish Catholics—Governor Hugh Carey or Senator Daniel Patrick Moynihan. No Democratic presidential race is really complete without a generous slathering of blarney.

PART V

Gentlemen, Place Your Bets!

Take calculated risks. That is quite different from being rash.
—*General George Patton*

Novice Cardplayer: Is this a game of chance?
W.C. Fields: Not the way I play it, no.
—*Scene from My Little Chickadee*

The sudden crisis following the seizure of the U.S. embassy in Teheran by a mob of student radicals created the usual surge of American patriotism in an emergency. National unity was the order of the day and, to a certain extent, rallying around the flag translated into rallying around President Carter. As long as the hostages were confined to limbo, Jimmy Carter's popularity was released from it. In the opening weeks of the crisis, his inaction was interpreted as calmness under pressure rather than helplessness. Coupled with Teddy Kennedy's lumpish performance on a number of early network interviews and his reckless, exaggerated denunciation of the Shah while the latter was still under American protection, the crisis at the outset gave Jimmy Carter a boost—in my opinion, an ephemeral one—in the polls. Kennedy's standing was correspondingly deflated.

However, none of this transient excitement drastically altered the long-term nominating picture. From the beginning it seemed almost inevitable that the climax to the embassy seizure and the holding of American hostages in Iran would either be violently tragic or drawn out to the point of anticlimax. Either way no one stood to gain significantly from the crisis in the long term, and any candidate foolish enough to try to manipulate it for short term gain was liable to hurt rather than help his chances.

As the campaign proceeds toward the conventions and the November general election, and as the economic discomfort index worsens, any foreign policy gains Jimmy Carter does make should be more than countered by dissatisfaction with his economic leadership—first benefiting Kennedy in the Democratic race and then, if Carter clings to the nomination, boosting Republican chances.

With this in mind let's look at the actual numerical ratings of each of the major contenders. My rating system is simple enough. Bakshian's Seven Deadly Whims *offers the ideal candidate a maximum score total of 100 points (barring any Wild Card pluses or minuses). The 100 point maximum total breaks down as follows:*

Whim 1 LEADERSHIP (a) Perceived . . . .   *15 points*
                        (b) Record . . . .   *10 points*
Whim 2 COMMUNICATION (a) Scripted . . . .   *10 points*
                        (b) Debate/Impromptu   *10 points*
Whim 3 ORGANIZATION . . . .   *20 points*
Whim 4 WAR CHEST . . . .   *15 points*
Whim 5 AGE/HEALTH . . . .   *10 points*
Whim 6 MARRIAGE/FAMILY . . . .   *10 points*
Whim 7 WILD CARD *(potential pluses or minuses*
                        of up to 10 points). . . . . .   *???*

Maximum Total (without Wild Card):. . . . . .   *100 points*

No flesh-and-blood candidate will ever score a full hundred points. But by rating each party cluster of candidates in descending order of individual scores we can establish not only their pecking order but the degree *of their differences in strength and standing. Remember: Candidate scores apply* only *to the race for their party's nomination. They can't be used to directly match Repub-*

licans against Democrats in a general election. As an example, because of his uniquely strong position as a frontrunner for the GOP nomination, Ronald Reagan has a higher score than either Carter or Kennedy, who are engaged in a much closer struggle for the Democratic nomination. That does not mean he would outscore either of them in a head-on match.

Let's examine the individual candidate charts by party, starting with the Democrats in the same order that they've already been written up in Part II.

JIMMY CARTER'S CHART

Whim 1 LEADERSHIP

    (a) Perceived   5

    (b) Record   5

Whim 2 COMMUNICATION

    (a) Scripted   5

    (b) Debate/Impromptu   8

Whim 3 ORGANIZATION   14

Whim 4 WAR CHEST   10

Whim 5 AGE/HEALTH   8

Whim 6 MARRIAGE/FAMILY . . .   8

Whim 7 WILD CARD . . . .   -2

CARTER TOTAL: 61

Points out of 100

TEDDY KENNEDY'S CHART

Whim 1 LEADERSHIP

(a) Perceived   8

(b) Record   6

Whim 2 COMMUNICATION

(a) Scripted   9

(b) Debate/Impromptu   4

Whim 3 ORGANIZATION   18

Whim 4 WAR CHEST   12

Whim 5 AGE/HEALTH   9

Whim 6 MARRIAGE/FAMILY . . .   6

Whim 7 WILD CARD . . . .   -8

KENNEDY TOTAL: 64

Points out of 100

JERRY BROWN'S CHART

Whim 1 LEADERSHIP
    (a) Perceived 6
    (b) Record 4

Whim 2 COMMUNICATION
    (a) Scripted 6
    (b) Debate/Impromptu 6

Whim 3 ORGANIZATION 6

Whim 4 WAR CHEST 4

Whim 5 AGE/HEALTH 10

Whim 6 MARRIAGE/FAMILY . . . 0

Whim 7 WILD CARD . . . . -6

BROWN TOTAL: 36

Points out of 100

Clearly the Democratic battle is a two-man race, with incumbent Carter a slight underdog to Teddy Kennedy (Carter scoring 61 points to Kennedy's 64), and Jerry Brown a mere nuisance factor at 36 points.

Translated into convention results, I see Teddy Kennedy nosing out Jimmy Carter and Jerry Brown coming nowhere near either of them.

Now to measure and match the Republican charts.

RONALD REAGAN'S CHART

Whim 1 LEADERSHIP
    (a) Perceived 8
    (b) Record 8

Whim 2 COMMUNICATION
    (a) Scripted 10
    (b) Debate/Impromptu 7

Whim 3 ORGANIZATION 18

Whim 4 WAR CHEST 15

Whim 5 AGE/HEALTH 5

Whim 6 MARRIAGE/FAMILY . . . 9

Whim 7 WILD CARD . . . . -5

                REAGAN TOTAL   75
                           Points out of 100

JOHN CONNALLY'S CHART

Whim 1 LEADERSHIP

    (a) **Perceived**   7

    (b) **Record**   3

Whim 2 COMMUNICATION

    (a) **Scripted**   8

    (b) **Debate/Impromptu**   7

Whim 3 ORGANIZATION   10

Whim 4 WAR CHEST   15

Whim 5 AGE/HEALTH   8

Whim 6 MARRIAGE/FAMILY . . .   9

Whim 7 WILD CARD . . . .   -8

                CONNALLY TOTAL: 59

                      Points out of 100

GEORGE BUSH'S CHART

Whim 1 LEADERSHIP
  (a) Perceived 5
  (b) Record 4

Whim 2 COMMUNICATION
  (a) Scripted 8
  (b) Debate/Impromptu 7

Whim 3 ORGANIZATION 15

Whim 4 WAR CHEST 10

Whim 5 AGE/HEALTH 9

Whim 6 MARRIAGE/FAMILY . . . 9

Whim 7 WILD CARD . . . . -1
                                    ___
              BUSH TOTAL: 66
                   Points out of 100

HOWARD BAKER'S CHART

Whim 1 LEADERSHIP

    (a) **Perceived** **10**

    (b) **Record** **8**

Whim 2 COMMUNICATION

    (a) **Scripted** **6**

    (b) **Debate/Impromptu** **7**

Whim 3 ORGANIZATION **5**

Whim 4 WAR CHEST **7**

Whim 5 AGE/HEALTH **9**

Whim 6 MARRIAGE/FAMILY . . . **7**

Whim 7 WILD CARD **0**

BAKER TOTAL: **59**

Points out of 100

Here we see an even clearer ranking than in the Democratic field, with Reagan a very strong frontrunner at 75 points, Bush his closest contender at a still distant 66 points and Connally and Baker vying for an equally trailing third place at 59 points each.

Translated into actual showings in the race for the nomination I read this as a likely Reagan victory—but one which has the "feel" of fragility about it. For this reason I would still pin a good longshot chance on George Bush to score an upset. Unless John Connally can drastically change his image and Baker can make miraculous organizational repairs in record time, I see neither of them surpassing Bush, much less Reagan.

This leaves us with the strong likelihood of Ronald Reagan facing either Kennedy or Carter, with Kennedy the slightly more likely of the two. Against Kennedy I believe Reagan would come fairly close but fail. With Carter as his sparring partner, I would give Reagan a nearly even chance of winning.

But what if Reagan is stopped on the way to Detroit? Numbers aside, I don't believe John Connally can do this, even if he does contribute to weakening Reagan along the way by rustling some of his conservative support in the South. However, Bush could, and even Baker might. More importantly, I am convinced that John Connally's negative reaction problem with the voters would lead him to defeat against either Carter or Kennedy. On the other hand, a unified party effort behind either Bush or Baker would have an edge over Carter, carrying most or all of the Western and Midwest states won by Ford in 1976 and capturing the necessary margin for victory in the South, which Carter cannot count on in 1980.

Against Kennedy, both Bush and Baker would have a harder time—say even chances with a well-balanced ticket, especially if it included a Catholic veep with some appeal in the urban Midwest and Northeast.

And if that isn't going out on a limb, please tell me what is.

Now for a last look at the campaign calendar to pinpoint

some early warning signals. On the Democratic side, Carter, who has already conceded New Hampshire and Massachusetts, must do very well in the early southern primaries (Alabama, Georgia, and Florida on March 11th—especially Florida). If Carter can sweep the field here he will more than have made up for his losses in New England. And if he goes on to win in Illinois on March 18th he will have captured the lead and transformed Teddy into the underdog.

My own hunch, though, is that Teddy might win in Florida and probably will win in Illinois. If he carries both, I'd say it's all over for Jimmy Carter. If Teddy only carries Illinois, it's still *probably curtains for Dogpatch on the Potomac. We'll see.*

On the Republican side, the Iowa caucus on January 21st will give the Reagan forces a chance to prove their claims to mass support and the Bush team an opportunity to flex its organizational muscles. If George Bush can run a close second in Iowa, he stretches his lead over Connally and Baker. If he upsets Reagan or comes precariously close to doing so, he also triggers a boom among the media and panics wavering Reaganites in other states, including New Hampshire. If Bush can again run second to Reagan in New England (the New Hampshire primary on February 26th, and Massachusetts and Vermont primaries on March 4th), he's strengthened his clear number-two placing and contributed to the decline of Baker and Connally.

Both of them in turn must do well against Reagan in the South just to keep their candidacies alive. For Connally, a fluke win in the March 8th South Carolina primary would be a help but not a safe conduct pass to Detroit. Unless he can also nose out Bush for second place in Florida, he could be finished before he gets to the Illinois primary.

And it is in Illinois that the whole thing is most likely to end. If Reagan carries New Hampshire and Florida comfortably and then wins in Illinois by a substantial margin, all that's left to be decided is the name of his veep. Only if Florida and

Illinois are close, or if Reagan is upset in one of them, will we see much real fighting for the GOP nomination after March 18th.

Thus the chances for an extended stalemate all the way to Detroit, resulting in a brokered convention choosing someone other than Reagan, Bush, Baker or Connally—most likely either Ford or Haig—are almost nil.

"The best of prophets of the future is the past," Lord Byron wrote in his journal a century and a half ago. The principle still holds. To the extent that my projections prove sound, it will be because they accurately measured trends and phenomena within our two major political parties that have been there to be seen for years. To the extent that they don't hold up, it will be due to my own misreading of those trends and phenomena—a failure to properly cast the 1980 set of players in the long-running drama of American presidential politics.

I am confident that much of this book will stand the test of events. If I weren't, I would never have bothered to write it. Still the only thing we can really be sure of in the 1980 presidential sweepstakes is an ancient truth from First Corinthians, *"They which run in a race run all, but one receiveth the prize."*

Envoi

*Together we must rise to ever higher
and higher platitudes.*
*—The late Mayor Daley of Chicago, Newsweek,
March 13, 1967*

IF YOU'LL EXCUSE me in a moment, I really must be getting to bed. Dawn is about to break on a bleak Washington winter's day, I've been writing all night and, worse yet, some criminal imbecile has planted a particularly ghastly long-playing record of nickelodeon music in the stack of Handel organ concertos on my phonograph. At the moment my weary ears are being bombarded by a mechanical violin/musical-saw rendition of "The Silvery Colorado," which has to be heard to be believed. Never mind. I'm too tired to get up and shut it off, and it'll be over in a moment anyway.

Except for this musical mishap, everything has ended rather neatly—my last page, my last glass of port and my last cigar are all about to expire in harmony. Two months ago, when I began work on this manuscript, I realized that I had stumbled onto a new if minor form of political writing. I call it "Pajama Journalism." For sixty days now, writing alone, late at night in my study, I have attempted to apply my grasp of the political past and my current first-hand experiences in the Congress, the Treasury, the White House and presidential campaigning to sorting out *The Candidates—1980*—writing about the future as history. All in all, it's been rather enjoyable, and I hope that some of the enjoyment has been passed on to my readers.

Karl Kraus, the great Austrian satirist, claimed that when people want to excuse some especially bestial lapse, they invariably plead that they're "only human." We sometimes tend to forget that politicians, too, are only human—though that may be giving a few I've known the benefit of the doubt. As Adlai Stevenson admonished, our public servants serve us right. The worse they are, the more they reflect our collective apathy, gullibility, greed or shortsightedness. That's how the worst of them get elected.

William Claude Dukenfield, better known as W.C. Fields, said it all when he said that you can't cheat an honest man. I believe the same is true of an honest electorate. Many people were fooled by Jimmy Carter in 1976 (possibly including Jimmy Carter himself) because they *wanted* to believe that his simplistic nostrums and transparent flattery of the average American were all we needed to make our country right again. Ditto Richard Nixon, Lyndon Johnson and John Kennedy; disillusionment in a democracy is never more than a few steps away from willful self-deception.

If this book has gone even a small way toward sharpening the critical faculties of American voters and heightening their awareness of how and why political parties nominate the kinds of people they do, it may have achieved some good. Whether or not it edifies, I do hope it has at least amused.

And so to bed.

—A.B.